Memories
OF LURGAN AND
OTHER THINGS

Memories
OF LURGAN AND
OTHER THINGS

GERRY CASEY

authorHOUSE®

AuthorHouse™ UK
1663 Liberty Drive
Bloomington, IN 47403 USA
www.authorhouse.co.uk
Phone: 0800.197.4150

Published by AuthorHouse 12/23/2015

ISBN: 978-1-5049-3624-8 (sc)
ISBN: 978-1-5049-3625-5 (e)

Dedication

This volume is dedicated to the people of Lurgan and its characters, of whom, there have been many both past and present and above all to the profound wit of Lurgan townsfolk, which is unique in itself and indeed has a character of its own that is inimitable and unsurpassed, rich and cultured in its diversity.

**"A proverb is the wit of one,
and the wisdom of many"**

Acknowledgements

The long arm of friendship and thankfulness is hereby extended to the people who have made this book possible and as the cliché states; this book would not have been viable without their help. The two main contributors are my Mother who provided me with a treasure trove of unequalled sayings and my sister-in-law Cathy, who has her own unique brand and collection of sayings. Their knowledge of sayings is immense. My appreciation is given to Fidelis Goldrick, who sent some beautiful verse and inspirational pieces.

GERRY CASEY

Introduction

This book is essentially a book of sayings and proverbs associated with the town of Lurgan in Co. Armagh and of its townsfolk, sayings that have been around for centuries and some which are still used in everyday speech to the present day. The main content of this particular volume will concentrate on the dialect and humor of Lurgan people and of the many varied forms of that humor. For that reason, it will not be necessarily one of a literary composition, but one of a sojourn to Lurgan of yesteryear and back again to Lurgan in the 21st Century.

Lurgan, like every other town and city, has changed dramatically during these years, yet it has amassed a rich legacy of wit and humor along the way, comparable to places such as Belfast, Liverpool or Glasgow, but still individualistic and quintessential of its people.

Lurgan, as they say, is Lurgan - inimitable in every sense of the word. The town has had its ups and downs but the character, wit and humor remains and is very much alive today. Indeed, it would be a sad loss to the town, if these qualities were to be replaced by a pseudo information technology form of humor, driven by megabytes and software.

Having said that, it would appear that the concept of virtual reality is here to stay and indeed the new technology has much to offer. In an ideal world, a subtle blend of the two cultures may counterbalance any discrepancy. Proverbs and the like contain rich pearls of wisdom and wit and sustain the character of the people much more than computers ever could - I would imagine! However, that is entirely the choice of future generations and one should not really stand in the way of progress and evolution, as they can bring their own rewards.

As well as the well- known and some not as well-known sayings and quips of Lurgan town, I have also included a selection of universal sayings which have stood the test of time and will hopefully remind the townsfolk that there is a vast world out there beyond the boundaries of their home town.

Finally, also included is a varied mix of eclectic material comprising a selection of poems (some written by the author), plus jokes, anecdotes, articles and worldwide sayings and catchphrases. Something for everyone, I trust!

Gerry Casey

The initials **GC** are those of the author and I have written some comments in relation to certain proverbs and sayings found in the book which will hopefully guide the reader.

THE FOLLOWING IS A SELECTION OF THOUGHT PROVOKING QUOTATIONS BY FAMOUS WRITERS, POETS, MUSICIANS ETC

The world is full of willing people. Some willing to work, and the rest willing to let them.
(ROBERT FROST)

Human behavior has always been I guess a matter of refraining from their work if someone is willing to do it for them. However, unemployment will always be around. **GC**

Modern Man in Search of a Soul.
(C.G. JUNG)

It would appear that the soul is a precious perhaps an elusive possession especially if modern man/woman is in search of theirs. **GC**

I just have thoughts in my head. I write them. I'm not trying to lend any causes for anyone else.
(BOB DYLAN)

I suppose Dylan was pointing out that he was no revolutionary. He just put his thoughts onto paper and through music and lyrics he was able to articulate them. **GC**

All good ideas arrive by chance.

(MAX ERNST)

One could sit all day and experience no such good ideas. But things happen in their own good time and ideas are no different. **GC**

The brain that doesn't feed itself eats itself.

(GORE VIDAL)

The brain is not like the stomach. Words and thought are its staple diet. **GC**

It gets harder the more you know. Because the more you find out, the uglier everything seems.

(FRANK ZAPPA)

I suppose the antidote may be that ignorance is bliss **GC**

Ye shall know the truth and the truth shall make you mad.

(ALDOUS HUXLEY)

Perhaps that's why there are fantasy films? **GC**

Truth like surgery may hurt, but it cures.
(HAN SUYIN)

Conflicting remarks indeed. However, the truth brings everything into the open and may rescue people. **GC**

No tears in the writer, no tears in the reader.
(ROBERT FROST)

I suppose the writer is king as they say. He/she must use a little magic to allow the reader to sense the writer's emotions. **GC**

To write poetry that does not rhyme is like playing tennis without a net.
(ALFRED LORD TENNYSON)

The poet is trying to say that this form of poetry is child's play and I agree to a certain extent because poetry that doesn't rhyme sometimes allows some poets to write beautiful stuff that otherwise they couldn't simply because of poetry rhyming which obviously restricts the writer to a degree. **GC**

Whether Invoked Or Not - God Will Be Present.
(C.G. JUNG)

Jung had many visions that involved God. Therefore, he assumed that God would be at his house whether invited or not. **GC**

The supreme reality of our time is our individual invisibility as children of God and the common vulnerability of our planet.

(J.F. KENNEDY)

Quite a mouthful here and I think the President was perhaps referring to the fact that some people were not overly concerned with God anymore but more about destroying the world rather than protecting it and that each nation was at risk from such consequences and the new extreme philosophies. **GC**

Every night I still ask the Lord – Why? - And I still haven't heard a decent answer yet.

(JACK KEROUAC)

I would imagine that that is the opposite of someone who believes yet doesn't need to see a sign of God's existence; they simply believe the word of God. Perhaps the void above encouraged Mr. Kerouac to go on the road with hippies in the sixties and he did write the bestseller On the Road as well! I think he was just looking for a sense of direction and having faith would have been the icing on the cake, if you like **GC**

Nobody can have the consolation of religion or philosophy unless they have first experienced their desolation.

(ALDOUS HUXLEY)

*I think Huxley may be saying that religion and philosophy are two concepts that incur desolation anyway and after that desolation and sense of not belonging to the real world, then there may be consolation when that state of mind has been experienced and processed either through religion or philosophy or both .***GC**

Never trust a man whose eyes are too close to his nose.

(L.B. JOHNSTON)

I think that L.B. may have been a little flippant when quoting and that the statement is more humorous rather than factual or scientific. **GC**

Life is what happens to you whilst you're busy making other plans.

(ROBERT FROST)

Here we have Robert Frost again and he is a great poet and thinker. The much regretted John Lennon used this line when he wrote a song for his young child Sean entitled Beautiful Boy form the album Double Fantasy shortly before John was assassinated in New York in 1980. How co-incidental was that? The quote means that you could be engulfed in something and be unaware that another thing could be happening simultaneously in tandem. **GC**

Two paths diverged into a wood. I took the path less travelled by. That has made all the difference.

(ROBERT FROST)

Finally, Mr. Frost again! I like this one and love to quote it! Choosing a road or path little used can make all the difference when one is at a crossroads in life. A bit like variety is the spice of life. If you are lucky enough you may choose the right path. Heads or tails! Good Luck! **GC**

"GENERAL QUOTES"

I loathe people who keep dogs. They are cowards who haven't got the guts to bite themselves.

(AUGUST SKINDBERG) - (DRAMATIST)

*I presume to be fair, that he may be referring to dangerous fighting dogs, or is he **barking** up the wrong tree?* **GC**

It's not where you come from. It's where you end up.

(VICTOR LEWIS-SMITH)

If you get the breaks needed you could end up rich, famous and happy. However, it's not that simple. Perhaps you end up where you were supposed to end up? **GC**

Do not use the word other. Help each other – don't condemn each other.

(SEAMUS HEANEY)

He is from my part of the world. He may be speaking about the divide in Irish politics. On the other hand, he may be speaking about people in general because where there are people, the word other(s) is usually prevalent. **GC**

Advice is something you give to other people, but something you wouldn't consider taking yourself.

(OSCAR WILDE)

Yes, it's very easy to give advice and more difficult to accept it. When you listen to people's problems, the problems appear insignificant from your point of view. So you may offer any kind of advice that springs to mind. However, turn the tables and this time you may turn down the help as the advice offered to you goes nowhere near to solving your mammoth problems, or so you think! **GC**

**Nostalgia is the realization
that things weren't as
Unbearable as they seemed at the time.**

**AN ASSORTMENT OF
LURGAN SAYINGS**

A know all, who knows nothing.
You never know what's in the
pot with the lid on.

I got it for a pig and a poke.
(To get a good deal)
Waste not, want not.
He fathers himself. *(The image of his father)*
It was bunged. *(A crowded pub or club)*
He's a fine fella. Any finer and he
would go down the grate.
Hiya Bourke/ Burke? *(I don't
believe a word you say)*
There's' no flies on him. *(He's no fool)*
Too sweet to be wholesome *(Not genuine)*
He's the born spit of himself.
(Referring to someone in a photograph)
He's better raving here than in bed.
(Someone talking nonsense)
I know every wheel of him.
(Knowing someone very well)

Do You
Remember?

A bucket on the stove boiling all the whites
The big tin bath on Saturday Nights
An old glass washboard, an outside loo,
Distemper on the walls, cardboard in your shoe.

Lino on floor, a scullery out the back,
A penny in the meter, coal brick coke and slack

Keys in the locks, door on the latch,
Long hot summers, ponies and traps.

Black leaded range, mansion red tiles,
Rag men, bone men who sharpen knives,
Ardglass herrings, buttermilk and snuff,
Soreheads, stomach aches, Tripe and onion
stuff.

Senna pods, Virol castor oil and malt,
A poultice for sore throats made of hot salt,
A half- moon water mark like a front door mat,
Soda farls and wheaten farls, cooling on the
rack.

Sheets made from flour bags. Winding up the
clocks,
Suspenders for men to hold up their socks,
Crombie coats, paddy hats, corner shops small,
Horse drawn hearses with black plumes tall.

Gas mantles, lamplighters, billycans of tay,
Walking home from dances, courting on the
way.
Fish and chips in newspapers, a pennyworth
of jam
A pound of broken biscuits, a trolly bus and
tram.

Donkeys hoof, pinade crocks, and beetles too.
Rinso Vim and soapflakes, newspaper in the loo
Carbolic soap, brylcreme, 7 o'clock blades
Sugar and water potion making permanent
waves.

Ale plants growing in a big sweetie jar,
Food safe with wire in every back yard
Hotspur and Rover, Dandy and Beano too.
A 3d, matinee or a jam pot in lieu.

A refund on a bottle, brown paper bags
Five Willie Woodbine or sharing half a fag
Hoops and cleeks and gliders, peeri whips
and all
Skipping songs, marbles, pitch and toss,
handball.

Top Twenty from Luxembourg, Desert Island
Discs,
Henry Hall Guest Night, rock and roll and twist.
Billy Cottons Band Show, A book at bedtime too
This list is never ending, but who the hells
'SKIBOO'!

A SELECTION OF UNIVERSAL SAYINGS THAT STOOD THE TEST OF TIME.

Love,
Marriage
And Romance

✧ A good wife and health are a man's best wealth.

I suppose the man could make more money if he is happy and healthy, and I think the message here is get a wife and prosper! **GC**

✧ All men are cavemen at heart, but some cave in faster than others.

A play on words here is evident. The cave man is the hunter gatherer but if he doesn't do a good job he will cave in! **GC**

✧ Marriage is an empty box. It remains empty unless you put in more than you take out.

It takes two to tango and if the said two do not work in unison and for the betterment of each other, the marriage may flounder and pay no dividends. **GC**

✧ Marriage is a woman's way of calling a meeting to order.

Perhaps she has him under a barrel now! **GC**

✧ A husband is a bachelor whose luck finally failed.

God help the cratur!

Nb: cratur is slang for creature and is mentioned in some American Western Movies and in Irish Speech e.g. the poor cratur. **GC**

✧ In some marriages, problems are all relative.

The term relative says it all. Keep it in the family! **GC**

✧ A woman either loves or hates; there is no alternative.

You got it! Her way or the highway! **GC**

✧ A man wrapped up in himself makes a very small parcel.

Not worth his weight in gold then? **GC**

✧ A woman could add years to her life by telling her true age.

   She's more interested in subtraction than addition! **GC**

✧ Home cooking is where many a man thinks his wife is.

   Maybe she is away fishing. **GC**

✧ A raving beauty is a girl who finishes second in a beauty contest.

   Try, try and try again. Next time, she will have form! **GC**

Parents & Kids

✧ Do not let your parents down; they brought you up.

   They brought you up; now make them proud of you. **GC**

✧ All adults need a child to teach; it's the way adults learn.

They wouldn't want to be without you; what would they do? **GC**

✧ Familiarity breeds contempt – and children. (Mark Twain)

I like this proverb equally as well as I like Mark Twain's work and humor. Your family can let you down. We all know that, yet blood is thicker than water which is a truism in its own right. Perhaps some people feel they can enjoy life better outside the confines of the home. Some think that they are under the microscope continually as far as family is concerned. There can be tremendous jealously as well in families; everyone trying to outdo each other which can result in such disappointment for some members. However, when the chips are down, families tend to rally around and support each other but not in every situation. A case of some do, and some don't. **GC**

✧ Choose your wife as you wish your children to be.

I suppose you choose your wife and know that your children will be a part of your wife and a part of yourself, the way it should be. So take your pick! **GC**

✧ Grey hair is hereditary – you get it from your children.

   That may be true to an extent. However, when you lose melamine from your hair whether you're 16 or 66, you will go grey. I get the children bit too! **GC**

✧ Child guidance is what more and more parents are getting from their children.

   There is a lot of truth in this as technology and the internet are ruling the waves and the kids are in the driving seat! **GC**

✧ many a little mug has grown to be a big pot.

   Watch and learn from others as the saying goes. Many big famous stores have shot up from nowhere and became household names such as Marks and Spencer's who began with a second hand counter! **GC**

✧ If you don't want your children to hear what you're saying, pretend you're talking to them.

✧ if you carry your childhood with you, you never become older. *(Abraham Sutzkever)*

Your childhood is your saving grace. If you still wonder at certain things which some people take for granted such as nature and get enjoyment from them, then it could be that your childhood is still an important thing in your life and worth treasuring. **GC**

✧ Teachers are never appreciated by parents until it rains all Saturday.

The last thing parents want is a rainy Saturday or worse still a wet weekend because all hell lets loose with all that pent up energy waiting to be released! Call for the teacher now! **GC**

✧ As the old cock crows, the young one learns.

Yes, I think that everything is passed down from parent to child especially in the early days and the animal kingdom is no different. It's a bit like the father passing down his skill or artisan to the children, assuming they wish that to happen. Keep it in the family as they say! **GC**

Husbands
&
Wives

The following is a clever take on the relationship between husbands and wives through wit, observation and joviality although there may be some sarcasm threw in for good measure!

✧ A man is incomplete until he's married – then he's finished.

A clever little remark, yet maybe the husband is better off now he's married, settled down and finished because he doesn't have to woo her anymore? **GC**

✧ A woman changes a lot after marriage, principally her husband's habits.

It's not so much her facial features but the way she runs the house and takes charge of what needs changing. If she has married a rich husband, then by all accounts she has landed on her feet! Enough said! GC

✧ Many a wife has turned an old rake into a lawnmower.

It's not so much that she has made him fork out for a new lawnmower, it's her way of telling him to get his act together and get mowing that lawn. 'poor wee cratur!' GC

✧ Nothing makes a woman think of things she's got to do in the house more than seeing her husband resting.

If he's sitting with his feet up watching the sport on the TV, that will never do, so she grabs the hoover, pushes the start button and commands him to give her a hand and up he obediently jumps. Game, set and match to the wee woman! **GC**

✧ shortly after marriage a man begins to realize that he has talked too much during his courtship.

Promises, promises! I'll get you this, I'll get you that! I'll get you the world. Now he has to live up to it and no messing about! Poor wee cratur! Self-inflicted! **GC**

✧ a woman in love is a very poor judge of character. (J.G. Holland)

Yes, the chemicals and hormones are flowing. Now she's back to earth, the garden doesn't appear that rosy anymore and the sky doesn't appear to be forever blue. I wonder why? **GC**

✧ Keep your eyes open before marriage and half-closed afterwards.

Perhaps this is a case taking everything in before marriage and half sleeping afterword's because it is too late then to pull out! Just accept it and pretend half the time that you didn't see what was annoying her? **GC**

✧ the only time a woman wishes she was a year older, is when she's expecting a baby.

A true saying if ever I heard one. No harm to the baby but the woman wants the birth done and dusted in order to get back to staying young once more. This baby lark is only a hiccup! **GC**

✧ The road to success is filled with women pushing their husbands along.

But of course! The wee man has to pull his weight, maybe three times his weight. According to the Missus things don't come easy if she wants top of the range cars, exotic holidays, expensive jewelry and a massive house and the little ole husband has to provide all this or else! **GC**

✧ A woman's chief asset is a man's imagination.

*Oh yeah, if the wee man has his eye on something either carnal or drink related or whatever, then he must pay for it. Get the readies out then! **GC**.*

✧ Most men who go through life with an enquiring mind, don't appreciate her.

*Yeah I like this. The enquiring mind in this case is the wife and she is the brains of the whole outfit, the one who never stops asking questions or figuring things out and profiting through it. The Einstein if you like! **GC***

Early poems from my collection.

Ambition

Where am I going, what have I done, It's time I had some fun,

When will it start, when will it end,

I'm going slowly around the bend,

Life is short, you have to begin to enjoy,

You're a man now, only once are you a boy,

But no more moaning, I'll start today,

And I'll have plenty to do and say,

I'll learn to drive, get a wife and settle down,

I'll wear a smile, no more a frown,

I'll get a job and learn to sing,

In a year or so, I will be better than Frank or Bing,

Someday I'll conquer this great big land.

Then I'll be someone and I'll stand tall and proud.

I'll stand on the rooftops and shout hard and loud.

Gerry Casey.

Swan of the Lake

Beautiful white swan gliding across the still lake,

A wonderful sight for people strolling in the busy park,

The young cygnets follow happily behind their proud mother,

The fleecy white feathers light up the view from the waterside, a vista not to be missed,

People come to watch and praise and offer food,

Other birds seem to stop and admire this majestic great swan,

For the swan is the sublime ruler of the lake, a creature like no other

Gerry Casey

The City

Traffic, crowds, noise and shoppers galore,

Another day in the city as people do their daily chores,

Fashion shops, supermarkets,

Butchers and corner café,

The business and industry of the city continues for yet another day,

How the city has changed in these hectic modern times,

The old Victorian church clock almost seems to know as it slowly chimes, acknowledging the times and taking register,

Yet cities change, if reluctantly decade by decade to keep up with the pace of life,

But the people rarely do as they preserve their keenness and determination for the city through all trouble and strife.

Gerry Casey

Honey Don't

Stop criticizing, splitting hairs, arguing, and meddling in my affairs,

Examine yourself; you may just see something amiss

What do you want? Money, gold, an exotic kiss,

You're hurting my pride, damaging my ego,

I still maintain my dignity, halt now, stop!

What about the good times we had together?

Have you forgotten me as well?

Treasure your memories; hold them to your heart,

It can all add up to a new exciting start,

Co-operation is the name of the game you see,

So try to imagine something new and forget about me,

Gerry Casey.

By the Seaside,

Summertime is here and people flock to the sea,

They come in their thousands as it's a popular place to be,

Parents swim in the sea as children play on the beach,

This is paradise on earth and away and from the city crowds,

The children smile as they enjoy their rock and lick ice cream as they frolic on the golden sands.

This is an idyllic scene and everyone is happy as they listen to the band merrily playing,

The crowds are happy on holiday and have a fantastic fortnight ahead,

They make the best of it, forgetting the cruel winter and the snow and ice.

Gerry Casey

Reflections

When we were young, we lived only for fun and the bright golden sun,

Problems were few, there was so much to do and happy things we done,

Now we've reached adulthood, things are different and life can be cold and hard,

Gone are our childhood days when we felt so daring and bold,

Everything was so easy then, we would listen to the chirping wren and run on the open countryside,

We would go to the inviting beach, away from the city's reach and on the donkeys we'd ride,

But alas, those wonderful peaceful days are forever in the past

We're men and women now and to our responsibilities we must run fast,

Our sentimental look into childhood days for ever gone was sweet,

But life calls us once more and we willingly go and do our utmost in good frames of mind

Gerry Casey

Notes… A space where the reader may wish to make a few comments or notes they would like to express on an individual basis for their personal use.

The River

Deep in the valley, the river flows on.

Through meadows and towns, on and on,

Great crested birds float on the river bed,

Making sure that their chicks are well fed,

Ardent anglers sit happily on the bank to fish,

The background roses out in flower so rich and fondant,

It's midsummer and the river is at its busiest as ever,

All kinds of wildlife one finds on a river,

The great river meanders through brook and pond,

Giving people so much pleasure and who are so happy to be a part of the great river.

Gerry Casey

Truth

We must seek the truth otherwise it will evade us,

What is truth, surely not just another word?

Will the truth set us free or imprison us,

Will it set us on the road to enlightenment or congest us into a cul de sac of confusion?

Definition of the word suggests honesty and liberation,

Instead of self- denial, it has the mechanism to was away our fears and tears,

Open new avenues, create new horizons and filter out our fears,

Once achieved, the sky is the limit, nothing is impossible, the world is our oyster. As great thinkers have said 'The truth shall set you free. It hurts but it cures.

No one should be afraid of the truth,

Better than any medicine, it has no side effects,

Natures' way of self- healing, no synthetic elements,

Derived from conscience and personality, the truth becomes a realization that truth is a panacea and the complete solution.

Gerry Casey

Notes… The reader may wish to jot down some thoughts or comments on above items.

Patience,
Kindness
& Good Manners

✧ the secret of patience is doing something else in the meantime.

This is very true I must say. If you are waiting for an egg to boil for example complete a little task you had in mind. If you wait on the egg boiling you will literally never see that egg boiling. Of course whilst you are completing the little task, keep one eye on the egg. Because if you don't the egg will be boiled dry. You can bank your bottom dollar on that! Always try to diversify in order to allow your patience to remain intact. Another example, if working on the computer, and waiting for something to download on a lazy computer, work on another task, then you should be content that you have 'killed two birds with the one stone! **GC**

✧ The test of good manners is to bear patiently with bad ones.

*If you are used to good manners, then it can be difficult to have to listen to bad manners. If the bad manners one has to put up with will be only for a brief period of time, then you should be able to withstand them. (**GC**)*

In the Wee Dark Hours.
Things that go bump in the night,
Incidences that give people a fright,
In the dark hours into the night,
People wait patiently for the morning light,

Passers- by make the old jitter and shake,
They turn for the light and lie awake,
Could it be a criminal or a rapist?
Or a petty thief or a mad sadist,

The world we live in can be very cruel,
We are forever in a combat of sheer duel so
the next time you think of the night,
Run like hell and hope no-one is in sight!

Gerry Casey.

You can't buy good manners, you either were given them from your parents or you learnt to cultivate them. **GC**

✧ Politeness is like a cushion; there is nothing in it, but it eases the jolts wonderfully.

A certain lightness reminiscent of floating through the air but has inner strength that is almost unbreakable. Such is politeness and it's free! **GC**

✧ Modern science is still unable to produce a better tranquilizer than a few kind words. – (Digest)

And the good thing is that a few kind words are not synthetic and have no side effects. If you behave as you would expect your friends to behave then kind words are all around you in big doses and you don't have to go to a chemist to receive them. So you're on a winner every time. **GC**

✧ He who receives most favors - knows how to return them.

Every good turn deserves a return because that is how the world revolves. He who takes all the time without return will soon lose out because he makes a name for himself, a name that pays no dividends. You do a favor for me and I will repay that favor because you were the first to do me a favor. It's so simple but is worth pointing out. **GC**

✧ The main aim of mankind should be to make men kinder.

I suppose that is why the term is spelt that way, mankind/humankind. Surely it is to make humankind appreciate their planet more and also the people who live on that planet. Most people have less than others but struggle on. A small percentage of people control the wealth, yet are reluctant to share it. The ideal is to make them aware that money isn't everything and there may be virtue and ultimate peace of mind to inherit if only they have a desire to change and help others. **GC**

✧ The smallest act of kindness is worth more than the grandest intention.

Good things come in small parcels as they say. Some people promise the earth but never deliver. Helping someone across the road means more to that person than for instance a friend invites a friend to their birthday party but fails to follow up and the friend is let down. *Kindness in small doses is worth more than a king's ransom.* **GC**

✧ there is no argument equal to a happy smile.

Charm will always win the day. You can always argue into submission. However, a genuine broad smile goes a long way. You don't need any force or persuasion. Just smile! **GC**

✧ be patient – the world is broad and wide.

Nurture patience, it is an indispensable gift. Sometimes it's difficult to sit and wait on the arrival of patience. Eventually it arrives and you are glad that you waited and everything has now come to fruition and now you know that the world is indeed broad and wide. **GC**

✧ of all the things you wear; your expression is the most important.

If you wear the richest and finest clothes that can be bought and don an unfavorable expression, then you might as well dress in rags as the gloomy expression overpowers the fine clothes. However, if you are dressed in rags and wear an attractive expression, then people do not see the rags but a happy person who is at ease with themselves because of their winning expression. **GC**

✧ The kindly word that fails today may bear its fruit tomorrow.

Chances are that the kindly word didn't get through because the person receiving it was unable for one reason or another to use it to good effect. Second time around the person offered the kindly word might be able to put it to good use because this time they know that it will reap benefits not just for the bearer but for those around them. **GC**

✧ The kindly heart is ever making silver linings for other people's clouds.

This person knows that the more you put in the more you take out because their joy is completed when the clouds dissipate and the sun breaks through, simply because the advice and love given has done the trick and the receiver is happy again. **GC**

✧ Take time to be friendly – it is the road to happiness.

Many good relationships begin with friendship. Therefore, to go out of ones way to be friendly will bear prosperity and a wealth of friendship all through life. You cannot choose your family but you can choose your friends who become a commodity richer than gold. **GC**

✧ the mind that is anxious about the future - is miserable. *(Seneca)*

I've heard it say that misery can be contagious and that it likes company. Perhaps but different people experience different events in their lives. It all depends where in the world one is either in a peaceful climate or where people are repressed or treated badly. However, to be blessed with a positive frame of mind definitely is an advantage as we go through life with its ups and downs. **GC**

✧ Kindness is a language, which the deaf can hear and the blind read.

If the language is spoken in a friendly way, the blind recognize that the giver is genuine and makes them feel at ease. The deaf can look at the giver and know instantly that the giver means every word that they themselves cannot hear but can interpret through the body language of the friendly person.

Education / Knowledge

✧ As long as you live, keep learning how to live.

I suppose it's a case of learning for life as the more you learn also means one never stops learning as new knowledge is constantly being updated especially in the social sciences field.

Again it's not only learning but you have to learn the proper way and that is learning how to live as the saying above illustrates. Having respect for each other is another valuable way of learning and one which eases the mind and promotes self confidence in the person. **GC**

✧ If you want a thing well done, do it yourself.

Only you know yourself a job well done is just that! If it is done to your satisfaction, then you are happy, If it isn't then you should do it yourself if you can. **GC**

✧ Tact will take a person further than cleverness.

You can be the smartest person on the planet but if you lack tact you may ruin everything. Knowing what to do and knowing what to say are real streetwise skills that have to be perfected because it they are not, no-one will take you serious as a business and social individual. **GC**

✧ everyone makes mistakes – that's why pencils have erasers.

The person who has never made a mistake doesn't exist. We learn through our mistakes. By tapping into these resources, we perfect the task in a professional and masterly way. Then we no longer fear our mistakes and if we get it wrong first time, we get it right second time around. **GC**

✧ A fool flatters himself; a wise man flatters the fool. – (Bulwer)

A fool may be too much in love with himself. He can't see the woods for the trees and will forever shower himself with compliments. The wise man will sing the praises of the fool and may receive a few dividends in return. The fool is none the wiser. **GC**

✧ People seldom improve when they have no other model but themselves to copy.

When people are so wrapped up in themselves, they usually can't see the length of their own nose and they invariably end up going nowhere. However, if they have a role model, they can escape their own skin and adopt the life of another whether the role model is a scientist or a famous sports person or a pop star. This can make all the difference because when one is 'acting' another person, the pressure is removed and the sky is the limit and success beckons. Then they can go back to being themselves when away from the limelight. **GC**

✧ A work of real merit finds favor at last. – (A.B. Alott)

A great piece of work will be discovered eventually. Lots of scrutiny and investigation will be applied to the work in order to evaluate if it is indeed a masterpiece. Then when everything seems lost, the work of merit will find favor among the scholars and academics and the rest is history as they say. Everything comes to those that wait. **GC**

✧ A perfectionist takes infinite pains and often gives them to other people.

A perfectionist is never happy even when he/she produces a masterpiece. It is really the Achilles heel of such an individual that nothing is right when everything is right. The people around them pay a big price in their quest to convince them that the work could be no better and is really unsurpassed in its own right. Sometimes it is a futile exercise in trying but in an astute way, the creator of the masterpiece knows that what is produced is a top class work of art! **GC**

✧ Never argue with your doctor – he has inside information.

This is a comical statement but makes a pertinent point. Everyone knows of course the 'inside information' means that your doctor has through the use of scans, and blood tests etc., an expert evaluation about your medical condition simply through the latest technology and professional knowledge he/she has at their disposal. You have of course a right to argue about your symptoms but little chance of disputing the evidence of technological breakthroughs in the medical field. **GC**

✧ Speak little about what you know and keep quiet about what you don't know.

You have to be quite diplomatic here. If you are well informed about a matter do not say too much about what you know if the matter is controversial or delicate as you could say too much and put yourself into a compromising position.

On the other hand if you are unsure about a matter that you know practically nothing about keep your mouth shut because that is wise counsel. **GC**

✧ Knowledge is of little use if it is not under the direction of good sense.

A little knowledge can be a dangerous thing if badly used and the consequences can be dire in that respect. Good sense must prevail in order for the knowledge to be utilized for the best and for common sense to prevail. **GC**

✧ Education is the apprenticeship of life. *– (Willmott)*

You cannot have an apprenticeship of life without education. An apprenticeship requires many skills and talents which have to be taught through a course of education to equip the trainee with lifelong skills. However, in reality education is the apprenticeship as it is gained throughout life every step of the way. **GC**

✧ Genius is one per cent inspiration and ninety-nine per cent perspiration.

The above statement is debatable as one cannot define genius. Of course you cannot put in one per cent inspiration and expect it to be a masterpiece. That is impossible. If you put in ninety nine per cent perspiration there is still no guarantee that the one per cent left will suffice. Perhaps a combination of the two might sway the balance but genius does not recognize percentages as genius. It could be argued that genius is born not made **GC**

✧ one of the finest accomplishments is making a long story short.

Yes when time is of the essence, this may be true as some people never get to the point and time is kicking on. This is where the listener or reader loses patience and may not want to hear any more of the story.

It may have been a great story but appears to have lost its gloss as the storyteller insisted on including finer details that were not required and in the process the teller went off on a tangent of some source.

However, if this story was a novel or a piece of renowned work, being brief would or may not be the proper approach. Then, the story requires to be told in an explanatory and piecemeal fashion leaving out no detail no matter how small or insignificant it appears to be. This is the work of a professional and the public arena may not be the showcase for his work.

In summary, telling a story to a friend or friends can be laborious to listen to and perhaps to tell a long story short may be the best option. However, in order to perfect a story properly, demands both time and patience away from the madding crowd. **GC**

✧ A wise man turns chance into good fortune.

This is one to ponder on. A wise man waits until the opportunity arises then pounces and prospers from it. He takes his chance when the going is good for he may never get another chance. **GC**

✧ Common sense is calculation applied to life. – *(Amiel)*

The writer may have been a mathematician as his choice of word calculation suggests. I would retort by stating that I think common sense is just using the brains that you are born with. **GC**

✧ A successful greengrocer is a man who knows his onions.

If he knows each and every one of his products then it follows that he knows his onions! **GC**

✧ Some people are never right, except when they admit they've made mistakes.

Some people think that they know it all even when they have been put right by people who only want to help them. Some people would argue that a black crow is white. That is an example of the extremes they will go to. **GC**

❖ He who waits shall get a parking ticket.

The message here I think is dwell too long and you will pay! If you want to get there fast go now or you'll never go. Do the job now or you will never finish it. The list goes on and on. If it is not car related, then do that thing now whether it is a marriage proposal or applying for a highflying job. **GC**

A COMPREHENSIVE
SELECTION OF
UNIVERSAL SAYINGS and PROVERBS

❖ Grow angry slowly – there's plenty of time.

Nobody wishes to be confronted by anger and there's plenty of it about. If we could find a panacea for anger, that would solve a lot of problems. However, anger is a human emotion just as love is and both are found in the psyche of the human being. The secret is trying to control such anger to an acceptable level. However, that is easier said than done. Anger management is thought to be quite effective in this regard and should be used more widely and should be encouraged. **GC**

❖ there's plenty of room at the top, but not for sitting down.

If you want to make it to the top, you must put every little ounce of energy into your quest to do so. Nothing must be spared and there must be no negative feeling or hesitation on the road to becoming a big success. If you believe wholeheartedly in yourself and hold tight to your positive thinking then you are truly on the road to riches and finding your deserved place at the top of the pyramid. Good luck! **GC**

❖ don't knock the weather. If it didn't change now and then, nine out of ten people couldn't start a conversation.

Oh yes, what would we do without the good old weather? It breaks every boundary or hindrance when we are gob smacked or speechless. You can't go wrong when the weather is the main topic of a conversation. Whether we are talking about stormy skies, brilliant sunshine or constant rain, it doesn't matter as the weather has won again as the supremo of all chat and conversation. Good day for it! **GC**

❖ Money doesn't just talk. It has the biggest audience.

Money is the route of all evil as they say. It speaks its own language; opens all doors and rules the world. If you have plenty of money, everyone loves you. If you haven't any; people ignore you. It creates jealousy, destroys character and makes you self-important and downright obnoxious. Yet everyone who is short of money rids it up but rarely declines it when offered. **GC**

❖ Co-operation, not competition, is the life of business.

When everyone works together for the success of the business as an enterprise, then all should share in the success and profit of the business. That way, one doesn't need competition among the workforce but co-operation in its place. **GC**

❖ Courage is not freedom from fear; it is being afraid and still going on.

This is the test of real character. Even though the person is petrified, there is something special in reserve which drives the individual onwards fearing nothing and no-one. These qualities only emerge when one is in extreme danger and the strong character within the person influences them to take a chance to complete his goal oblivious to all around him. **GC**

❖ Be master of your habits or they will master you.

If you have the self- confidence to control your habits and if they are seemingly insignificant or major then you should be ok in that regard. However, if you let your habits run loose and you do not put continuous effort into keeping them under control, then they will undoubtedly master you and who knows what calamities you have let yourself into! **GC**

❖ Credit - is a way of making cheap things dear.

Spot on! If you are one who refuses to pay interest, then you won't consider credit because you don't need to. However, for people who have insufficient funds one way or the other, paying no interest is not an option. Then you enter the trap of the dreaded credit! **GC**

❖ cut your own wood and it will warm you twice.

It's your wood now and you will enjoy it even better. It's a bit like cooking your own meals. You have done the hard work and it will taste even better, because of it. That's not to say that someone cooking the meal for you is not appreciated. They are but if a time comes when you are left to your own devices then you should be quite capable. The same applies to cutting the wood or any household task that requires doing. **GC**

❖ we know what happens to people who stay in the middle of the road – they get run over. – *(Aneurin Bevan)*

This is a case of not trying enough when carving out a living or becoming a success in life. If you stand in the wings or look on sheepishly, then life may pass you by and you could end up resentful or bitter. If you do put an effort in, you could surprise yourself with the success you achieve and when success is enjoyed, then generally people want more! **GC**

❖ When you're dog-tired at night; maybe it's because you've growled all day.

Could be or it could be the opposite. Growling all day might keep a body awake all night but little or no growling may result in sleeping like a baby. Your guess is as good as mine! **GC**

49

❖ No matter what you do, someone always knew you would.

   A very common retort is when someone says; I always knew you would do that someday. Perhaps they receive similar platitudes? **GC**

❖ my idea of happiness is four feet on a fireplace fender.

   Yes, it's a warming thought! **GC**

❖ it's not the years in your life – but the life in your years that counts!

   It's no use totting up 100 years in your life without remembering a good portion of them as great vibrant brilliant times. If they were boring and uneventful years then surely they weren't even worth remembering them? A positive person lives life to the full but a negative person keeps life at bay and comes across as defensive and wary. **GC**

❖ If all economists were laid end to end, they would not reach a conclusion. - *(George Bernard Shaw)*

Too many great thinking minds rarely agree or equate with each other. They have too many thoughts churning over in their minds. If you asked a hundred psychiatrists for a diagnosis each one would differ. **GC**

❖ Some people complain because roses have thorns; be glad that thorns have roses!

Perhaps it's because of the two extremes? Thorns are rough and painful to the touch as if they are there to detract visitors and also to protect the gentility of the sacred rose. You could say that a certain amount of suffering has to be endured before we see the true beauty of the rose in its splendor after the thorn has permitted entrance by giving in to the fragrant rose. **GC**

❖ Fortune-teller reading customers palm – "You're a very gullible man!"

When one is desperate or down in luck they will try anything. However, some fortune tellers are very accurate in their predictions. Perhaps we should see it as entertainment? **GC**

❖ after dinner, rest awhile; after supper, walk a mile.

The above quote is good thinking. There is so much wisdom and advice especially regarding health matters. The biggest meal of the day is one's dinner. Because it is a large meal, it takes quite a while to digest the contents of it. Therefore, rather than work it off, you are advised to have a rest or even a little nap!

Your supper is the last meal of the day before you go to bed. In this instance, you are better advised to work it off with exercise or go for a long walk because your stomach may be rather full. Worse, you would not wish go to bed and just lie there as you may end up having negative feelings or even nightmares as when all is said and done, the bulk of the meal should not be still in your stomach but well digested to prevent the above things occurring. **GC**

❖ leaving no stone unturned can sometimes ruin the path.

If you go too far in trying to settle matters it could be that you ruin everything in your path. If you adopt a policy of leniency things may work out so well that you didn't think it could be possible. Choosing a degree of subtly and reverting to a method of a happy medium far out ways a barnstorming attitude. You wouldn't use a sledgehammer to crack a nut would you! Use your common sense! **GC**

❖ don't stare up the steps – step up the stairs.

This is another example of standing in the wings. There is little point in staring up the stairs if you have no intention of going to the very top. If you immediately step up the stairs, then you could be on the road to success and riches! Once you have negotiated that first tentative step up, you have accomplished something big. Step by step you will grow more confident and feel so much more self-assured. When you reach that final step and cross the threshold, you have arrived and what a beautiful feeling that is! Success is yours for the taking. So grab your chance as if you may never have that chance again. Congratulations on a job well- done my friend! **GC**

❖ know the true value of time; snatch, seize and enjoy every minute of it.

Time waits for no-one so they say. It can pass away so swiftly almost without a trace. To live a packed and full life, you have to grab the opportunities whilst they are available, otherwise they will be gone as others will surely snatch them away from you. Before you know you will if lucky, have amassed some brilliant memories of time past, simply because you have taken your chances and succeeded while others didn't and faltered. **GC**

❖ He, who only thinks of number one, should remember that it is next to nothing.

The term number one immediately conjures up connotations of selfishness and of a person only looking out for themselves. They may have many possessions and vast riches but in reality they have nothing as they have failed to share in any of their conquests in making money with the result that their money is meaningless and the owner finds misery and not human comfort and love which money cannot buy as that comes from the heart and the soul. **GC**

❖ Selfish people usually get everything they want, except happiness.

Selfish people are driven by selfish deeds. They generally don't care who gets in their way as they will crush those people who do.

At the end of the day, they have 'the world' but lack happiness. **GC**

❖ A consistent man believes in destiny, a capricious man in change. – *(Disraeli)*

A consistent man is usually of a conservative mind set, content to wait around until he encounters his destiny. A capricious man is restless and doesn't have the time to wait on destiny. Instead he desires change no matter what that change is. He is prepared to act on his word and beliefs irrespective of the consequence. He wants his people to be awarded the benefits that other prosperous people enjoy and the fruits of his labor will be equality and fairness for all in the immediate future. **GC**

❖ People do not lack strength, they lack will.

Strength is a formidable weapon at ones disposal. However, that is never enough. To achieve your goal in life, you need more. The most important ingredient has to be will. If you lack will, no goal or desire will ever be fulfilled. Once you embrace the quality of will, you are already there. The rest will follow almost automatically and you will have reached your goal and all because of your will. **GC**

❖ if you owe a bore a dinner – send it to him.

Send it as quick as possible because you will not be able to suffer another of his infamous dinners where he talks consistently about subjects that you do not have the slightest interest in. **GC**

❖ Happiness happens to people too busy to be miserable.

If we keep ourselves busy and live life to the full, we won't have time to be miserable. They say that misery likes company. If so, keep it at bay and give it no space as it may surround you with sorrow. Look out for the bright things of life and you should not go far wrong. Treat happiness as your friend and misery as your enemy as no good things emanate from being miserable. **GC**

❖ Middle age is when you start eating what is good for you, instead of what you like.

During youth, young people usually get away with eating anything they wish simply because they have strong bodies and internal organs which operate efficiently and perform at the highest level. Come middle age and the owner of the middle aged body becomes more precarious of what he/she is putting into their bodies. It is not a question of analyzing every food substance but being careful and selective in choosing the proper diet. One usually finds that if they treat their body system with respect and do not go overboard in the eating stakes, then through a happy medium attitude, they too can enjoy a healthy lifestyle like their youthful counterparts. **GC**

❖ Anyone who goes to a psychiatrist - ought to have their head examined. - *(Sam Goldwyn)*

Sam was famous for his roundabout sayings yet still came out with hilarious comments such as this one. When you go to see a psychiatrist you literally get 'your head' examined and Sam was quick to get on the bandwagon of ironic situations and even had a genre of funny remarks named after ham, thus the famous Goldwynisms. **(GC)**

❖ I never think of the future. It comes soon enough. - *(Albert Einstein)*

When you look back on life from a certain age standpoint, one realizes that life is short and you wonder where those lost decades went. Five minutes sometimes feels like five years depending on how much you are enjoying the moment! Yet a decade or even half a century just whizzes past and still the years are counting up. I have heard the saying from the older generation advising us that you should take the good from the morning as the afternoons are short. Such good advice and which falls into the wisdom that Mr. Einstein is displaying. A final saying is that life is too short for arguing or fighting amongst people. (GC)

❖ when trouble goes to sleep, don't set the alarm clock.

The above quip suggests that someone is forever creating trouble in the household. I'm sure that there is a little element of tongue in cheek about the whole affair! However, when he or she gets off to sleep, it is probably a good idea for everyone concerned that the alarm clock is not set because there is an excellent chance that 'trouble' will oversleep and that the entire household will experience true bliss in every sense of the word! **(GC)**

❖ A friend to everybody – is a friend to nobody.

Anybody's dog for a bone as we say in Ireland. Everybody needs a friend but a friend that they can call upon if and when they need them. A person who is always there assuming they have the time because we can't always impinge on peoples time. But in essence a friend is someone they can trust and able to listen to their troubles and woes.

The other side of the coin is a fair weather friend who lives for kicks and is forever helping themselves at the expense of the person who considers them to be loyal and trustful which very often they are not.

If a so-called friend has friends in double figures then they are only imitation friends because they would not have the time for friendship and secondly they will only avail of such friends when they know that there is something in it for them. Such friends are not real friends but parasites who live off their friends and that is to be frowned upon unfortunately. **(GC)**

❖ The Evening News is where they begin with *"Good Evening"*, and then tell you why it isn't.

An old ally of the above is where when there is no news then they make it up. I wouldn't say that is the gospel truth if you like. However, there has to be news either bad or good or both. The news industry is reliable on people making news mostly through crime and when 'breaking news' is flashed onto our screens you can bet your bottom dollar that such news is rarely good.

At the tail end of the news there may be a celebrity piece to soften the blow of a serious news item or a good deed story or something else. Yet everyone wants to hear the news and I suppose that means that news reporting is universally popular. **(GC)**

❖ anybody who isn't pulling his weight is probably pushing his luck.

There is always someone or others benefitting from someone's hard work either in the workplace or society in general. Some or keen, some are not too keen. There is a fool born every day who eases the load of others by honestly working hard and thus impressing the boss. However, invariably the fool doesn't reap the awards. The one who slacks in his work may be efficient in other ways. Step up the chatterbox he of slick talking and so called charm and charisma. He will usually be the one who receives the trophy on behalf of the team. He will take the plaudits and smile every step of the way. The fool and others like him will remain the hard working colleagues of the luck pusher. Perhaps one day, the tide will turn and the hard workers will be recognized as such and the trickster found out? Wishful thinking do I hear you say! **(GC)**

❖ if you are sitting on top of the world, remember it turns over every twenty-four hours.

The world is forever turning and thus life's circumstances and the pecking order changes with it. One minute you are top of the world, the next, you hit rock bottom. Therefore you can't rest on your laurels as your achievements are fleeting and gone as fast as they arrived. You can't take anything for granted and you have to keep up with the latest technology and marketing in a huge global world. Remember you are only as good as your last brilliant idea because as you are celebrating it, there is no doubt that a new one is poised to replace yours! That's the way of the world. **(GC)**

❖ Compassion will cure more sins than condemnation.- *(Ward Beecher)*

If the sinner is aware that there is compassion on offer, there is an excellent chance that they will embrace it rather than shun the help available.

If a wrong doer is forever condemned by the powers that be, then he or she will see little sense in conforming as the condemnation seems static and harsh with little sign of love or warmth.

Rather than punish the offender, would it not be better to encourage them and to treat them like any other human being. They should be introduced to the system and offered a role so that the person feels wanted and sees themselves as a respected member of the community. That way, there will be no reason to condemn but to congratulate them on their decision to change and make a valid contribution to society in general. **(GC)**

❖ He, who laughs last, probably intended to have told the story himself. *('600' Magazine)*

❖ Treasure your time; don't spend it, invest it.

This is an interesting proverb. Time is precious as they say. Treasure it and learn from it. The more time spent learning from it enables one to succeed in life not only from their chosen career but in learning about people and places. It is wise to travel even if some of us are not seekers but home birds as travelling broadens the mind because the world is full of interesting people and amazing places situated in every corner of the globe. The mornings are sometimes slow but the afternoons are quick. And time waits for no-one as the song reminds us. **GC**

❖ A word from a friend is doubly enjoyable in dark days. - *(Goethe)*

When dark days of winter or darkened spirits arise in a troubled soul, a friend getting in touch offering a kind word or a shoulder to cry on is riches indeed. Someone to share the load or sit by the fire and chat about bygone days cheer up the person who is feeling low and in need of a true friend whose trust is genuine and beyond approach. Not only is the receiver blessed with friendship but also can confide in one who is respected and treasured. **GC**

❖ Stand for something, or you'll fall for anything.

People generally ought to make their mind up and devote some time to a cause or something in order to make life more enriching instead of jumping on the band wagon and therefore believing everything that is literally thrown at them. A cause may give meaning to life and get oneself out of their hum drum life and the result can be spectacular. However, that cause has to be specific and carefully chosen otherwise they may support every endeavor known to humankind and therefore fail to specialize in their chosen quest. It is a case of throwing every ounce of energy into their pursuit and making that cause worth seeing through. **GC**

❖ An old timer is one who remembers when charity was a virtue and not an organization.

People, even the most genuine and trustworthy people, are in today's world *ever suspicious that some charities are not the charities of old or in fact charities at all. Almost daily there are reports on the media and in the press of charities and individuals who are accused of misappropriating funds. It appears that nothing is sacred anymore. People are now through frustration and anger returning to another belief that charity begins at home rather than trust individuals whom they don't know and therefore the givers are reluctant to donate because of the adverse reputation of so- called charities globally and instead are giving any left over money from their hard earned wages to the up keep of their families and rightly so. **GC***

❖ God made just a few perfect heads – the rest he covered with hair.

*This is perhaps another example of many are called but few are chosen. There is another implication here that it takes an exceptional person to carry the weight if chosen as the burden would be assumed as heavy with all the troubles of the world laden upon strong shoulders and wide backs as if God has chosen his special disciples who have the back to carry the burden as told in biblical times. **GC***

❖ Go to bed thankful and wake up hopeful.

If we believe in an entity more powerful than ourselves, then we have the capacity to be thankful. Knowing and believing in that promise strengthens us and we can wake up hopeful. **GC**

LURGAN LINGO

WORK
(WOARK)

The following sayings are written here in the local Lurgan dialect

A great wee woarker (*worker*)
Are ye toiling?(*are you working?*)
He's fascinated by work, he cud stand and watch it all day!
The divil makes work for idle hands.
Working moves (*someone up to fly tricks*).
he cuddn't bate snow off a rope.

He wuddn't woark in a fit
He thinks manual labor is a Spaniard.
This page and some other pages contain Lurgan dialect which is quite different from American or British English!

A story circulating around Lurgan one time was that yer man was on the *'Bru'* (which is a slang word for Bureau of Employment) for so that long that the staff sent him a Christmas Card each year. One New Year's Eve, he was invited to the *'Bru's big Do'*. At the end of the evening, they all sang to him, *"Will ye no come back again?"* The Manager sang an encore, *"Will ye definitely NO come back again!"*

Singing

He cuddn't sing to keep himself warm.
He sounds like a cracked record.
Hasn't an air.
He wud waken the dead!

Money / Meanness

He cud paper the walls with five-pound notes.
I wish I was a pound behind ye.
She wuddn't pay her maker.
She wuddn't give ye God's daylight.
I wish I had yer oul sock.
He wuddn't spend Christmas.
He wuddn't buy ye a drink if yer tongue was touching the town clock.

He wud rather fall on a knife than buy you a drink.
He hasn't two ha'pennies to rub tagaa.
There's not a saft joint in im. (He's no fool)

Character / Identity

Everybody's dog for a bone.
As many faces as the town clock.
He'd buy ya and sell ya.
As cunning as a fox.
He's no mug.
Knows more than his prayers.
More in his head than a comb wud take out.
Silly go saftly.
Not as slow as he walks aisy *(easy)*.
Takes a wise man to act the fool.
God help his wit.
God help im, he hasn't an ounce.
He's lived before *(a crafty one)*.
Slippy Tit *(a crafty one)*.

Explanation of an
'Olde Lurgan Saying'.

An old phrase I used to hear, when I was growing up in Lurgan and which in fact I still hear today was when for example, someone remarks on the weather, especially when it is bad or atrocious. They often say, "The waa's cat!"

I always wondered where the term 'cat' originated. I knew for a fact that it wasn't of the feline variety! Recently, would you believe it, I discovered the true meaning of it, in a short story in **"Ireland's Own",** a long-standing family magazine dedicated to folklore. Apparently the word 'cat' is an abbreviation for catastrophic – meaning disastrous. I never imagined for one instance that I would find an explanation for it. As they say, "Everything *comes* to those who wait!"

The following are all sayings and quips that have been heard in *or* around Lurgan throughout many years and over many generations.

Some *are* self-explanatory – others may need careful interpretation! I shall leave it up to the readers to draw their own conclusions!

All of the sayings are in verbatim form and spelt as in **local Lurgan dialect.**

Miscellaneous

- ✦ Long runs the fox.
- ✦ There's wiser locked up.
- ✦ There's a long road with no turning.
- ✦ Six years is not seven.
- ✦ What's done is done.
- ✦ Are you going up Blough?
  (High Street in Lurgan was referred to as Blough by older generations).
- ✦ Put a beggar on horseback and he'll ride to hell.
- ✦ He's not as bad as he's blackened.
- ✦ You're a blow!
- ✦ He's as cross as two sticks.
- ✦ The least said, the easiest mended.
- ✦ Two wrongs don't make a right.
- ✦ He's anybody's dog for a bone.
- ✦ I'm ready for the long ward with my hair cut.
- ✦ He hasn't a titter of wit.
- ✦ He has a neck for anything but soap.
- ✦ All duck or no dinner. *(no half measures)*
- ✦ He wuddn't give ya God's daylight.
- ✦ Ya cuddn't bate it with a big stick!
- ✦ A new broom sweeps clean, for a while.
- ✦ God made the back for the burden.
- ✦ He's as useful as a chocolate fireguard.
- ✦ Every dog has his day.
- ✦ He's not backward at coming forward.

✦ A face like a Lurgan spade.
  (A famous saying heard far and wide)
✦ More faces than the town clock.
✦ You never miss the water till the well runs
  dry.
✦ House Divil, Street Angel.
✦ Gone but not forgotten.
✦ There's no smoke without fire.
✦ What's sauce for the goose is sauce for the
  gander.

GENERAL LURGAN QUIPS
(With translations in brackets
where appropriate)

He's like a rat peeping out of a yard brush.

(Not good-looking, perhaps also has a moustache).

He has a face like the back of a bus.
(When buses were distortedly constructed –
saying in the 50's and 60's).

Are ye talking to me or chewing a brick?
(I can't understand what you're saying).

Like a bear with a sore head. - *(To be in a bad mood).*

He'd start a row in a cemetery. - *(An agitator, fighter).*

His bark is worse than his bite. - (Full of hot air, not the worse).

He's like chewing gum, sticks to my shoe. - *(Clinging kid).*

He would go through a brick wall for a short cut. *(Determined, doesn't hang about).*

He'd charm the birds' aff the trees.

"The writers' job, in a way, is to celebrate and criticize his own community in equal measure.– (Bernard McLaverty – Author of CAL, LAMB).

GENERAL LURGAN QUIPS
(With translations in brackets where appropriate)

The flure's that clean, ya cud ate your grub aff it. *(A sparkling floor).*

Not a smitch on it. - (A *clean* item of clothing).

Don't throw off a clout till the month of May is out.
(A famous universal saying clout in this cose means vest or something similar).

Say nothing till ye see Gallery.

(Gallery was a solicitor in Lurgan who was very much respected and valued especially among the underprivileged, uneducated people of the town).

The blind leading the blind. - *(Total confusion).*

What way are ye getting to the match?
Answer: "I'm going by Shanks Mare", i.e. "I'm walking".

Neither chick nor child. - *(A spinster).*

I went to the High School on the Hill. I met the scholars coming back.

The Rule of Thumb: An explanation:
An 18th century term, when apparently
a man was not permitted
to hit his wife with an implement
no wider than the
width of his thumb!

Word has it that there is a character residing in Lurgan who has a unique and unrivalled skill of actually peeling an orange in his pocket whilst wearing boxing gloves! The said character is not perceived by the townsfolk of the town to be mean or tight-fisted, only that he has an innate ability to perform such a task.

We have searched high and low to identify this individual, but he refuses to come forward. It seems he is publicity shy and doesn't welcome fame and notoriety. To save his blushes and to celebrate his incredible dexterity, we award him a place in Lurgan's Hall of Fame under the section of Anonymous.

A QUESTION / ANSWER SESSION AMONG TWO LURGAN PEOPLE

Q.	Well, how ye keeping?	(Are you well?)
A.	I'm not too bad.	Hinging taga
Q.	And yerself?	
A.	Ach! Hinging taga	*Together (Doing rightly)*
Q.	And the missus?	

A.	*Ach! Doing rightly.*	(Probably won the pools)
Q.	**Are ye going anywhere this year?**	
A.	*Na!Cuddn't afford it.*	(*She's* definitely won the pools)

MORE LURGAN SAYINGS FROM THE PEOPLE OF LURGAN

- ♠ Pay peanuts get monkeys. *(Cheap Staff)*
- ♠ The eyes are the windys to the soul.
- ♠ Gods ways are not ours.
- ♠ People in glasshouses shouldn't throw stones.
- ♠ Nothing on them or in them. *(The Poor)*
- ♠ Blood is thicker than water.
- ♠ Patience is a virtue.
- ♠ It's always darkest before the dawn.
- ♠ Where there's life there's hope.
- ♠ Where there's a will, there's a way.
- ♠ Out of adversity springs eternal hope.
- ♠ You scratch my back, I'll scratch yours.
- ♠ your money or your life, your tobacco or your pipe.
- ♠ He's no dozer. *(No fool)*

• Windys - Windows

Notes/comments……

+ Grass doesn't grow on a busy street.
+ Don't judge the book by the cover.
+ He hasn't an ounce. (*No sense*)
+ One man's meat is another man's poison.
+ Ye can lack it or lump it. (*It's up to you!*)
+ As sound as a pound.
+ As straight as a die.
+ No mun, no fun.
+ We git on like a house on fire.
+ Lack gitting blood out of a stone.
+ I wasn't born yesterday. I was born the day before.

A SELECTION OF JOKES AND HUMOUROUS ANECDOTES HEARD AROUND LURGAN PAST AND PRESENT.

GAME FOR CHICKEN?

A young lad currently unemployed was on the lookout for a job. He was approached by a friend who was a supervisor in the local Moy Park factory.

The supervisor was a wisecracking sort. *"If I got you a job here",* he cracked, *"You wouldn't chicken-out would you?"* The young lad laughed. The supervisor continued, *"It wouldn't ruffle your feathers if you got the job? I mean you wouldn't go cold turkey on me, would you?"*

YOUR MONEY OR YOUR LIFE!

Back in the 50s it was reported that a Lurgan man had accidentally swallowed a half-crown during a bout of unabated prolonged excitement. The frantic wife managed to rush him to the spec (hospital), where he was sedated and admitted. After he was settled, she was instructed to go home and telephone later about her husband's condition.

Later that evening she rang from a coin-box telephone. When she managed to put the money in, she was put through to the doctor in charge. *"What about him?"* she enquired breathlessly. After a long, drawn-out pause, the doctor replied solemnly, *"Well, there's no change out of him".*

My Canine Friend.

My pet dog is a great friend and I'll love him
to the end,
When I'm with him, I'm never alone,
I bring him gifts like a huge bone,
We go for long walks, like to the park,
He lights my world up like a candle in the dark,
If he went away I'd be the loneliest in town,
Because when he's around, I'm always up,
never down
They say man's best friend is a dog and it's true,
He always makes me very happy, and never
sad or blue.

Gerry Casey

Human Resources

When the chips are down and defenses low,
What must we do, accept defeat or begin
aglow?
Strengthen muscles, assert the sinews, and
keep to the fore,

Resources are plentiful, search for that inner
strength, our capabilities are galore!
The human being is not designed to wither
and die,

But made to celebrate to sing, adore and rejoice not sigh,
Out of adversity, springs eternal hope and good cheer,

Someone to care for; someone to call dear.

Gerry Casey

Notes.......The reader is invited to write notes where appropriate when a space presents itself. This can be an opportunity to personalize their copy if they so wish GC)

FACTORY TALES

A few commands from the foreman to the raw new recruit who unwittingly carries them out:

"Could you fetch me a bucket of blue steam?"

"Go down and get me a glass hammer".

"Go down to the office and ask for a long rest".

WORK - Digs not up to scratch

In the early 1960s, a Lurgan man went to England in search of work. Whilst in lodgings, he complained to the landlady about fleas in his bed. The landlady taken aback by such accusations, vehemently protested. *"How dare you!"* she howled. *"There is not a single flea in this house".* As quick as a flash and with profound Lurgan wit, her lodger quipped, *"No, yer right, they're all married with large families!"*

Arriving in the Promise land.

Another Lurgan man also travelled to England, hoping to find work. Having just disembarked from the boat, he bought a daily paper. Looking at the front-page headline of the paper, he immediately thought that his search was over, even before it had begun. *"I cud be lucky here"*, he thought. By the way, the headline was as follows: - *"400 JOBS IN JEOPARDY!"*. So, he thought he would call into a nearby pub to enquire. On entering the pub, he confidently shuffled up to the counter. Looking the barman straight in the eye, he pleasantly asked him, "Hello, excuse me. Cud ye give me directions to Jeopardy?" The barman, puzzled to say the least, muttered, *"What do you mean sir?"* The Lurgan man replied innocently, *"I heard there was 400 jobs in Jeopardy".*

SOME POPULAR SLOGANS
(Dates Included)

Access – your flexible friend.	- *(1981 onwards)*
And all because the Lady loves Milk Tray	- *(1968 onwards)*
Australians wouldn't give a XXXX for anything else.	- *Castlemaine Lager - (1986 onwards)*
Beanz means Heinz - *(C. 1967)*	
Been there. Done that. Got the T-shirt.	- (Been there done that recorded from 1980s
	Expanded form from 1990s)

American Express?.......... That'll do nicely, Sir.	*- (1970s)*
Bovril..........Prevents that sinking feeling.	*- (1920)*
Can you tell Stork from Butter?	*- (C. 1956)*
Clunk, Click, every trip. - Ad promoting seatbelts.	*- (1971)*
Crime doesn't pay	*- A slogan of the FBI + Cartoon Detective Dick Tracy.*
The Customer is always right- from French - Le client n'a jamais tort.	
(literally, "The Customer is never wrong", coined by Cesar Ritz 1850-1918)	
Does she...or doesn't she? - Clairol Hair Colouring.	*- (1950s)*

Don't be vague – ask for Haig	*- (Haig Whiskey C.1936)*
Don't forget the fruit gums mum!	*- (1955-61)*
Full of Eastern Promise - Ad for Frys Turkish Delight	*- (1950s onwards)*
Go to work on an egg	*- (1957 onwards)*
The Greatest Show on Earth - Barnum & Baileys Circus	*- (1880s)*
Guinness is good for you	*- (1930s)*
Happiness is a Cigar called Hamlet.	*- (1970s onwards)*
Have a Break, have a Kit-Kat.	*- (from C. 1955)*

Heineken refreshes the parts other beers can't reach.	*(1975 onwards)*
I am a Marxist - of the Groucho tendency.	*- (Slogan found at A'anterre in Paris 1968)*
If you want to get ahead, get a hat.	*- (ad Slogan for Hat Council U.K. 1965)*
I'm only here for the beer. - Double Diamond Beer.	*(1971 onwards)*
It Beats as it Sweeps as it Cleans. - Hoover Vacuum Cleaner.	*- (1919)*
It's Finger Lickin Good.	- Kentucky Fried Chicken - *(1958)*
It's Good to Talk	*- B.T. Ad - (1994)*
Make Love – Not War.	*- Student Slogan - (1960s)*

A Mars a Day, Helps you Work, Rest & Play.	- (C. 1960s Onwards)
Let your Fingers do the Walking.	- Yellow Pages (1960s onwards)
Keep That Schoolgirl Complexion. - Palmolive Soap	- (from 1917)
Kills all known germs	- Domestos Bleach -(1959)
I was a Seven Stone Weakling	- Charles Atlas ad U.S.A.
Just when you thought it was safe to go back in the water.	
Featuring the return of the great white shark.	
- Ad copy from film Jaws 2 - (1975)	
The Mint with the Hole	- Polo Mints Ad - (From 1947)

My Goodness, My Guinness	- *(1935)*
Nice one Cyril - Ad for Wonderloaf	
Adopted by fans of Cyril Knowles, Spurs Footballer - (1972)	
Nothing over sixpence - Woolworths Stores U.K.	- *(from 1909)*
Oxo gives a meal man-appeal	- *(C 1960)*
Persil Washes Whiter – and it shows.	- *Persil. - (1970s)*
Pile it High. Sell it Cheap.	- *Tesco Supermarkets Slogan*
(1898-1979)	
P-P-P-Pick up a Penguin	- Penguin Chocolate Biscuits
(C - 1970s)	

Put a Tiger in your Tank	*- ESSO, USA.- (1964)*
The Right One	- Martini, U.K. - (1976)
Say it with Flowers	- Society of American Florists.
Sch.....You Know Who.	- Schweppes Minerals. - (1960s)
Snap! Crackle! Pop!	- Kelloggs Rice Krispies - (C 1928)
Someone, Somewhere, wants a Letter from you	*- Post Office Ad- (1960s)*
Stop me and buy one	- Walls *Ice*-Cream - (from 1922)
Things go better with Coke	*- Coca Cola - (1963)*

Top Breeders Recommend It	- *Pedigree Chum Dog Food Ad* - *(1964)*
You're Never Alone with a Strand	- Ad for Strand Cigarettes- (1960)
We're Number Two. We Try Harder	- Avis Car Rentals

A LOCAL RESIDENT, JIM LENNON, KINDLY SUPPLIED THE FOLLOWING INVENTORY, WHICH IS A FAIRLY COMPREHENSIVE LIST OF LURGAN DIALECT MANNERISMS.

DIP	BLEACH
CLASHBAG	TELL TALE
RIFT	TO BELCH OR BURP
JAW TUB	KITCHEN SINK
FERNENST	FACING YOU
CRIBBEN	KERB OR KERB STONE
SWATTERED	PERSPIRING, SWEATING
IN GUTTERS	RATHER DIRTY
MITCHING SCHOOL	PLAYING TRUANT

DROOTH	VERY THIRSTY
SLOAT	DRINK OR GULP
SLIDER	ICE-CREAM – WAFER
POKE	ICE-CREAM CONE
FOUNDERED	FREEZING/VERY COLD
BOGGING	FILTHY/DIRTY
CRABBING	BAD TEMPERED
TO CLASH A DOOR	SHUT FIERCELY
GLIPE	A STUPID PERSON
SLABBER	LOUD MOUTHED PERSON
CLIESTER	UNTIDY WORKER OR PERSON
WINDY STOOL	WINDOW SILL
LOODERING	BEATEN UP
HAVING ONES HEAD SHOWERED	GETTING A MINUTES PEACE.
IT WOULD CUT YOU	VERY SHARP COLD WIND
NOT A ROOSICK	POOR/NO MONEY
TO BLURT	BURST OUT CRYING
GUB OR COOTER BOX	FACE
CLODDING	THROWING STONES
BOKING	GAGGING/VOMITING
STORN CHILD	DIFFICULT/UNRULY CHILD

LASHING	POURING DOWN WITH RAIN
CLART	UNCLEAN/DIRTY PERSON

AWAY AND DAVART[1]
YOURSELF   GO AND PLAY

JAPPED	MUD SPLATTERED AS IN FOOT WEAR
SPARAFART	RUNT OR SMALL PERSON
CRIGGED TOE	STUBBED YOUR TOE
STOTIOUS	VERY DRUNK/ INEBRIATED
CODDING	JOKING/MAKING FUN
BARGING	SCOLDING
SHILLCORN	SPOT/BLEMISH/ PIMPLE
NOT AT YOURSELF	FEELING UNWELL/ SICK
STANDING IN MY LIGHT	BLOCKING MY VIEW
	OR STANDING IN THE ROAD *(Same meaning)*

---

[1] DAVART PROBABLY MEANT DIVERT!

TONGUE NEVER LAY	NEVER STOPPED TALKING
HOWL YOUR WHIST	JUST A MOMENT
BEELDING	A FESTERING SORE

LURGAN DIALECT
e.g. "we had the quare oul times of it".

Definition of dialect. The dictionary initially describes dialect as a form of speech peculiar to a certain region. Secondly, that it is a subordinate variety of a language with non-standard vocabulary, pronunciation or grammar. Lurgan has its own distinct 'language' as most regions do. A certain percentage of its dialect has been 'borrowed' from other places as some of it has been introduced by people who have come to live in the town over the generations going back, perhaps hundreds of years.

CHATTERBOXES

Once he starts, there's no stopping im.
Talk till yer blue in the face.
Talk till the cows come home.
He's got the gift of the gab.
He'd talk the hind legs aff a donkey
She'd talk the horns aff a goat.

FOOD / GREED

All duck or no dinner.
Making a beast of imself.
He wants his cake and eat it.
Porridge will put hairs on yer chest.

An older persons description
of spuds. (potatoes)

They're like balls of flour.	*(good potatoes)*
They're like balls of water.	*(bad potatoes)*
It's like porter. You cud stand on it.	*(a poor cup of tea)*
He would live in yer ear	*(meaning a parasite)*

"Diary of a 'Long Suffering' Lurgan woman recorded in speech to her loved ones".

She's having wee dwarms	(Little bouts of illness)
She's also not at herself	*(She's not feeling well)*
My heads splitting	(She has a headache)
I'm dying	(She's not well)

I'm drawing my last breath	*(She's tired)*
I've never had a pain lack it	*(She's constipated)*
I'm a martyr for pains	*(She has a bad back)*
I'm ready for the long ward	*(She's 32 and tired)*
I'll swing for yez	(Threatening suicide, but only short of housekeeping money)
I'm not able to walk	(Just before she goes to bingo)
What I've suffered!	(She's just got over the flu)
The Doctor told me I hadn't long to live	*(The Doctor told her*
to come less often as his patient quota has increased)	
I can't go to the toilet	*(She went 10 minutes ago)*
I haven't had a bite all day	*(She's had a box of Diary Milk, a Snickers and Six French Fancies)*

EPISODES OF EVERYDAY LURGAN SPEECH
AS TOWNSFOLK GO ABOUT THEIR DAILY ROUTINES.

Imagine the scenario as two people have a chat in a local shop or on the street.

"What about im?" "Ah, he's not too well". "Still the same?" "He kin hardly move, but ya cuddn't talk to im. He wuddn't listen. There's no bidding in im". "Did ya go out on Saturday night?" "Oh, I went to the club". "Many there?" "It was bunged. Ya cuddn't get moving. I left early". "I see yer man came home last night, as drunk as a monkey. Cuddn't bite his own thumb! He was gassed and talking oul nonsense. If he had brains he'd be dangerous. A know all that knows nothing! There's wiser locked up. *But* ya cuddn't tell im. He knows it all. God help his wit! *But* he got the quare gunk1 as there was nobody to listen to im. He had to talk to imself. God help the cratur".

[1] - Gunk means surprise, shock

GREED / WANT

➤ The full man does not or wants to understand the wants of the hungry.
➤ Poor men take to the sea, the rich to the mountains.
➤ Poor is the church without music.
➤ The thief is no danger to the beggar.
➤ It's a good story that fills the belly.
➤ Sharp is the eye of a hungry person.
➤ Good humour comes from the kitchen.
➤ A blessing is no good to a starving person.
➤ One cannot take out of a sack more than what's in it.
➤ Honey is sweet, but don't lick it off a brick.
➤ A king's shilling is no more than a poor man's farthing.
➤ Too many irons in the fire.
➤ A finger in every pie.
➤ What is rent to a lord, is food to a child.
➤ The bottle is half full not half empty…

Triads

Triads are a form of traditional Irish sayings that date back to centuries long past. They are arranged in groups of three. The Welsh also used triads in literary compositions.

The following are a selection of popular and enriching triads, which contain such gems of wisdom.

Three things most difficult to select:
A woman, a scythe and a razor.

Three assets of a woman:
A broad bosom, a slender waist and a short back.

Three great things of life:
Sunshine, wisdom and generosity.

Three kinds of men:
The worker, the pleasure-seeker and the boaster.

Three worst endings:
A house burning, a ship sinking and an old white horse dying.

Three things that don't have rest:
A steep waterfall, an otter and a devil out of hell.

Three truths:
Sunrise, sunset and death.

Three useless things when old:
An old schoolmaster, an old horse and an old soldier.

Three things that come unnoticed:
Rent, age and a beard.

Three strange forces:
Fire, water and hatred.

Three happiest in the world:
The Tailor, the piper and the goat.

Three pair that never agree:
Two married women in the same house.
Two cats with one mouse.
Two bachelors after the one young woman.

Three sweetest melodies:
The churning of butter.
The plough ploughing.
The mill grinding.

Three sauciest by nature:
A Ram.
A Bull.
A Tailor.

A few quotes on the subject of writing

I have come to this resolution, never to write for the sake of writing or making a poem, but from running over with any little knowledge or experience, which many years of reflection may perhaps give me – otherwise I shall be dumb.

(John Keats) (1795-1821)

A poet is the most unpoetically of any- thing in existence, because he has no identity, he is continually in for – and filling some other body.

(John Keats) (1795-1821)

✄ HAIR DISPLAY

Findings of a Questionnaire sent out to Lurgan residents asking why there are so many hairdressers in the Lurgan area. Here are just some of the more popular replies!

✄ Well, they all get their wee cut.

✄ Hair today, gone tomorrow.

✄ You could perm any 6 from 8.

✄ It's a cut throat business.

✂ When it comes to business, it's a close shave.

✂ They are head and shoulders above every other business.

✂ Their staff report that they enjoy good fringe benefits.

✂ They all appear to gel together.

✂ Well, that's the long and the short of it!

Health & Fitness

He's a shadow of himself.
He's awful failed.
Lucks lack death warmed up.
A picture of health.
A tight wee man.
He lucks mended
He's put the weight back on.
Yer luckin good.

He's away up the town like a lilty.* *(origin unknown)
As fit as a fiddle.
He's a wirey wee man.
She wuddn't see ya in her way.
(a fit woman)

Dishonesty & Deception

🔨 He wud sink ye in a spoonful of water.

🔨 I wuddn't make fish of one and flesh of the other.
(Make no difference, especially between sons and daughters).

🔨 Give him an inch and he'll take a mile.
(Preying on another's kindness and generosity)

🔨 He'd steal the flies from a blind spider.
(a skinflint, having no scruples or standards)

Local Colloquialisms
(Written in an ad-lib mode)

He's as thick as two short planks.	He's a holy terror.
Money dis'nt buy happiness, but it will do till happiness comes.	Gimma head pace.
	I cuddn't tell ye.

Better the divil ye know that the one you don't.	Your man cud tell ye.
Money goes to money.	Quit your codding!
It's a dead loss.	A dacent wee cratur.
There ye are now.	A nice wee sowl.
Ay - dead – on now.	Wuddn't harm a fly.
Tell us anaw one.	An obliging bugger
He's an odd cratur.	*(open to interpretation – basically means helpful)*
He's as odd as tay.	
He's quare crack.	Good meat for each aw.
Ye big eejit.	Who rattled your cage?
He's a real head-bin.	If he had brains, he'd be dangerous.
Didee by jove?	A watching kettle never boils.
Holy Smoke!	

MAKING JUDGEMENT

If there's a hole in your coat, they'll make it bigger. - *(exaggerating someones faults)*.

You're a blow! – (meaning a 'big head'. Someone who tells tall stories or is on an ego trip).

A short scenario to explain an
old Lurgan term "drooth" –
meaning a terrible thirst.

He comes down in the morning, a bedraggled wizened figure. *"I've a powerful drooth on me!"* he growls to the wife. *"Anything to drink?"* Relaxed and unperturbed, she whispers in a soft tone, *"What like?"* *"Anything"*, he blethers in a piercing voice. *"Well"*, she says in a tone similar to the female rabbit in the chocolate ad, *"you have three choices - turpentine, last weeks porridge or yesterdays milk!"*.
"Is that all?" he mutters almost inaudibly.
"Well", she replies, slightly purring in an ultra relaxed fashion, "I'm not rockafella. Beggars can't be choosers. Money doesn't grow on trees, especially on the halfpenny side of the street". Enough said.

SKY

See the clear skies, that unobtrusive
light,
A bird on the wing
Sheer delight...
Penetrate the clouds, look for that
Silver lining
Reach for that fiery ball,
glimmering, shining.
The world is your oyster
Touch and feel,
Tender to the touch, yes
It's Real.
These things for you,
they cannot be bought.
All experience and knowledge,
neither can be taught.
Heavenly bodies twirl and reel
Each holding their own mysteries,
Turning, yet on an even keel

Gerry Casey

A Poem about the Linen *Industry*.....

The Linen Mill

Crash, Rattle, the weaving of looms sound,

And to another long, hard day,
the workers are bound.
The men and women happily spin their yarn,
While the sewers settle down
and get ready to darn.
In its heyday, the mill was the
chief industry of the town,
Now sadly, its' on the short road down.
People no longer need linen as
much as years gone by,
They now have a whole new
range of materials to try.
Generations of men, women and
children have worked in the
mill,
Now due to new industries and
careers they no longer will.
Weaving, spinning and darning
are all trades of the past,
For the industrial revolution
has come on fast.

Gerry Casey

LURGAN ONE-LINERS!

Catch yourself on!
That's sticking out!

Did the jab rightly!

He did indeed!
Ye wuddn't know!
There ye are now! *(said in a
slow exaggerated fashion)*
She was cat!
The town's packed!
Ye cuddn't get moving!
There's no flies on im!
I'm away for a bottle!
I'll go for a dander! - *(A stroll)*
Drunk as a monkey!
Aye right - dead on!
God, ye wuddn't know im!
Haven't see im in ages!
Disn't luck imself!
He and yer man's right and thick!
- *(Friendly with each other)*
She's a holy terror!
Never shuts up!
Tongue never lies! - *(Non-stop talker)*
Buy and sell ye!
Coming and going all day!
She's up and down lack a yo-yo!
Never off batter! - *(Busy body)*
As many faces as the town clock!
Tell a lie to get ya hung!
Wuddn't believe a woard she says!

Tell ye anything!
A bad hide! - *(Toublemaker)*
A real Commotionist!
A nice wee man when he's sleeping!
He'd sleep the clock round!
Wuddn't give ye nothing!
Haven't got me head showered all day!
No rest for the wicked!
Nothing else for it!
A tongue on her that wud cut iron!
Had the place in an uproar!
There's wiser locked up!
He'll never die in his bed!
How ye keeping?
What about ye?
Long runs the fox!
Ye cuddn't lend me a fiver?

Cheer up, it's only 8 months to Christmas!
I remember the sun splitting the stones!
It wud freeze ya!
It wud cut ye in two!
I feel a wee spit cumming on!
A draught lack a step-mothers breath!
There's good drying the day!
I haven't got a minutes pace!
I'm hardly able to walk!
As fit as a fiddle!
Cuddn't keep up wee ya!

The following is a verse discovered on a tombstone in Baltimore USA, centuries ago. It has been immortalized from then on and is as popular today as it ever was……

DESIDERATA

Go placidly amid the noise and haste and remember what peace there may be in silence. As far as possible, without surrender, be on good terms with all persons.

Speak your truth quietly and clearly and listen to others, even the dull and the ignorant; they too have their story.

Avoid loud and aggressive persons; they are a vexation to the spirit.

If you compare yourself to others, you may become vain and bitter, for always there will be greater and lesser persons than yourself, enjoy your achievements as well as your plans.

Keep interested in your own career however humble; it is a real possession in the changing fortunes of time. Exercise caution in your business affairs, for the world is full of trickery.

But let this not blind you to what virtue there is; many persons strive for high ideals and everywhere life is full of heroism.

Be yourself; especially, do not feign affection, neither be cynical about love, for in the face of all aridity and disenchantment, it is as perennial as the grass.

Take kindly counsel of the years, gracefully surrendering the things of youth. Nurture strength of spirit to shield you in sudden misfortune, but do not distress yourself with imaginings; many fears are born of fatigue and loneliness. Beyond a wholesome discipline, be gentle with yourself.

YOU ARE A CHILD OF THE UNIVERSE:
NO LESS THAN THE TREES AND THE STARS
YOU HAVE A RIGHT TO BE HERE
AND WHETHER OR NOT IT IS CLEAR TO YOU;
THE UNIVERSE IS UNFOLDING
AS IT SHOULD.

Therefore, be at peace with God, whatever you conceive him to be and whatever your labors and aspirations in the noisy confusion of life, keep peace with your soul.

With all its sham, drudgery and broken dreams, it is still a beautiful world. Be cheerful; strive to be happy.

Comment: this wonderful poem/statement has stood the test of time and some people actually live their life around the captivating verse and richness of the overall simplicity twinned with down to earth common sense.

I am confident that generations upon generations will find comfort in the advice offered through this great epitaph. **GC**

If
by
Rudyard Kipling

If you can keep your head when all about you
    Are losing theirs and blaming it on you;
    If you can trust yourself when all men doubt you,
    But make allowance for their doubting too:
    If you can wait and not be tired by waiting,
    Or being lied about, don't deal in lies,
    Or being hated don't give way to hating,
    And yet don't look too good, nor talk too wise:

If you can dream - and not make dreams your master;

    If you can think - and not make thought your aim,

If you can meet with Triumph and Disaster,

    And treat those two impostors just the same;

If you can bear to hear the truth you've spoken

    Twisted by knaves to make a trap for fools,

Or watch the things you gave your life to, broken,

    And stoop and build 'em up with worn-out tools:

If you can make one heap of all your winnings

    And risk it on one turn of the pitch-and-toss,

And lose, and start again at your beginnings

    And never breathe a word about your loss;

If you can force your heart and nerve and sinew

    To serve your turn long after they have gone,

And so hold on when there is nothing in you

    Except the Will which says to them: 'Hold on!"

If you can talk with crowds and keep your virtue,

    Or walk with Kings - nor lose the common touch,

If neither foes nor loving friends can hurt you,

    If all men count with you, but none too much;

If you can fill the unforgiving minute
    With sixty seconds worth of distance run,
Yours is the Earth and everything that's in it,
    And - which is more - you'll be a Man, my son!

The Business of Life

If life is getting you down and you need a quick pick-me-up have a look at this inspirational piece from a *Victorian* periodical.

Look on the bright side. It is the right side. The times may be hard, but it will make them no easier by wearing a gloomy and sad countenance. It is the sunshine and not the cloud that makes the flower. There is always that before or around us which should cheer and fill the hearts with warmth. The sky is blue ten times where it is black once. You have troubles, it may be. So have others. None are free from them. Perhaps it is as well that none should be. They give sinew and tone to life-fortitude and courage to man. That would be a dull sea, and the sailor would never get skill, where there was nothing to disturb the surface of the ocean. It is the duty of everyone to extract all the happiness and enjoyment he can without and within him, and above all he should look on the bright side of things.

In the long run the great balance rights itself. What is ill becomes well-what is wrong, right. Men are not made to hang down either heads or lips; and those who do, only show that they are departing from the paths of true common sense and right. Cultivate what is warm and genial-not the cold and repulsive, the dark and morose.

A thundercloud looks dark and terrific at a distance, but when it approaches near it assumes a lighter appearance and passes off, leaving the heavens calm and delightful. Thus it is with the difficulties of life. Seen at a distance, they are large and formidable. It seems impossible to surmount them. With faith and courage we press on, with a steady eye and a strong heart, and what appeared like mountains before has dwindled into mole hills.

The business of life is to go forward. He who sees evil in prospects, meets it in his way; but he who catches it by retrospection, turns back to find it. That which is feared, may sometimes be avoided; but that which is regretted today, may be regretted tomorrow. We should, to be careful, decidedly condemn the indulgence of brooding over circumstances and events that thought cannot mend, because it unstrings the mind; and that once done, it is surprising with what rapidity all its peace unravels itself; and how much it loses of the power of judging rightly on the mixed condition of human affairs.

Courage then, courage! Rise with the determination never to sink again, nor sit despairingly beneath the harrow of despondency. With this resolution your work is half accomplished. Success will follow in your track.

AGE ACCORDING TO LURGANITES

He's as oul as the hills.
She's no chicken.
Sha must be 70 if shiz a day.
He's not able for it now.
Ye ken see im gittin oul.
??? Shiz dun.
??? He lucks his age.
??? He's as grey as a rat.
??? He can hardly walk.
??? Over the hill.

113

???	Badly on his feet.
???	She's years oulder than me.
???	I was only a young girl at school when she was woarking out.
???	Well up in years now.
???	Not gittin any younger, lack miself.
???	Showing the years now.
???	Gittin on now.
???	Disn't luck a day over 30.
???	Well into his seventies.
???	Hasn't changed a bit.
???	Still lucks the same ta me.
???	He must be a powerful age.
???	I'm ready for the long ward.
???	Trying to act the young fella.
???	No respect for their elders.
???	When ya git oul, nobody wants ye.
???	I've a spring in me step.
???	She's lived before.
???	Well done up.
???	He's long on the go.
???	A craking door lasts long.

AND THERE'S MORE....

❖ When ye get up in the morning to put on ye, ye don't know whose taking aff ye at night.

❖ A smile and a wee bit of civility goes a long way.

❖ Gods good and the divils not bad!

❖ Speak no evil, see no evil, hear no evil.

❖ There's wiser locked up.

❖ Better knowing the divil - than the divil you don't!!!

❖ Butter wuddn't melt in his mouth.

❖ We all stand on the shoulders of giants. *(meaning we all learn from each other)*

❖ It cud happen to a bishop.

❖ Catch yerself on!

❖ It's all in his hat.

❖ As honest as the day is long.

COLOURS AS SEEN THROUGH THE KALEIDOSCOPE OF LURGAN LIFE.

- ♦ Black as yer boot.

- ♦ Whiter than white.

- ♦ As green as grass.

- ♦ As grey as a rat.

- ♦ Argue a black crow white.

- ♦ Red as a beetroot.

- ♦ Not as green as he's cabbage luckin.

- ♦ I near torned porple. *(Purple)*

- ♦ He lucked rale yella luckin. *(Yellow)*

- ♦ As brown as a bottle of buttermilk.

  (A sarcastic Lurgan remark when someone has returned from holiday abroad)

- ♦ As black as the ace of spades.

  (Well, Lurgan is spade town?)

- As white as a sheet. *(Not looking well)*

- As brown as a berry. *(Sporting a good tan)*

- Lack a yella dockin. *(Dockin, probably a dock plant)*

- Talk to yer blue in the face.

- Everything that glitters is not gold.

EVERYDAY PHILOSOPHY FROM EVERYDAY PHILOSOPHERS.

Forty is the old age of youth – fifty the youth of old age.

He's not a complete fool, some parts are missing.

A tax collector has got what it takes to take what you've got.

Two things that don't go down well – running upstairs and running down people.

It feels better when other people point out your good qualities without your help.

The vandal does his best to do his worst.

God sends the food – the devil sends the cooks.

According to a tennis player – 'love' means nothing.

The trouble with being on time is that there is no one there to see you.

Don't put off until tomorrow what you can put off until next month.

Why do too many cooks spoil the broth if many hands make light work?

A rolling stone gathers plenty of money.

Why is there always too much month left at the end of my money?

We are all cast in the same mould but some are mouldier than others.

Sometimes I wake up grumpy, at other times I let him sleep.

The trouble with being retired is that you never get a day off.

Rome wasn't built in a day – it just looks that way.

I wasn't born yesterday – I was born the day before.

Express yourself and get yourself into hot water.

It doesn't rain but it pours.

Teachers who have poor vision can't control their pupils.

"WORDS ARE, OF COURSE
THE MOST POWERFUL
DRUG USED BY MANKIND." Rudyard Kipling

'LURGAN' MONEY
- A CURRENCY OF A BYGONE AGE –

Thruppeny bit - worth 3 old pence often referred to as a 'Portadown Washer'.

Quid - a pound note.

In Australia a half-wit is called as 'one who is not the full quid'. Lurgan people say: 'not the full shilling'.

Perhaps there is a connection there! Sayings are transported to other lands and sometimes distorted or converted to suit other dialects.

A Dollar- proper name - a half-crown worth 2 shillings and sixpence.

2 Bob - a florin – worth 2 shillings.

A Bob - a shilling – worth 12 old pence.

A Halfpenny - worth half an old penny.

A Tanner - a sixpence worth six pennies.

A Farthing - worth a ¼ of an old penny.

The Penny itself - a large bronze coin worth a twelfth of a shilling and associated with many old sayings. A popular Lurgan one was – '*I haven't a penny to ma name!*'

MONEYPENNY

'In for a penny, in for a pound'.
- Meaning total commitment to a task.

Like a bad penny. - Always turning up when unwanted.

Pennies from heaven. - An unexpected windfall.

Penny Black.
- The 1ˢᵗ adhesive postage stamp (1840 – worth one penny).

The Penny Drops.
- When a person finally understands the situation.

Penny Farthing.
- An early bicycle with one large wheel and one small one.

A Penny for your thoughts.
- To reveal your thoughts to an observer.

A Pretty Penny. - *A large sum of money.*

Two a Penny.
- Plenty in circulation, e.g. a small business, However, not worth a lot!

I'm Forever Counting Bubbles!

Have you ever wondered how many bubbles make up the head of a typical pint of

Guinness? Well, I contacted Nick McGuinness of, wud you believe, Guinness Brewery. This is his account to me, told over the phone in rapid, quick fire fashion!

The purrfect pint of Guinness should be served with a compact, creamy head on it, which should, preferably measure between 10 and 15 mm. The proper way to serve it is to employ the two-part pour. Fill the glass to ¾'s full, leave to settle before a final top-up. If you are the creative type, a shamrock motif on the head is recommended, but not compulsory, and it requires great, dexterity and a steady hand!

Assuming that the head on our superbly served perfect specimen of a pint is the average, say 12.5mm and for the eggheads among us who are aware that the average bubble size is 50 millionths of a metre, then there should be (after a quick calculation), 300 million individual bubbles that go to make up the head.

That by anyone's reckoning comes to more than 78 bubbles per head of population of the country as a whole or to put it another way a single bubble for every adult (over-18) in the European Union.

For punters who normally avail of the two part pour, they do appreciate the ample time it gives to anticipate the serving of the pint and of the satisfaction of watching it settle.

However, to actually count every individual bubble would be to defeat the issue! Just drink and enjoy!

Wise Words from Worldwide Stars

"Men can starve from lack
of self-realization,
as they can starve from a lack of bread".
Novelist Richard Wright.

Food is important. However, humankind need more than food as they need spiritual nourishment for their souls and bodies as they go through life. Food will keep the body ticking over. However, people need encouragement and love and attention which come from other people around them. If they are artists, be it writers, musicians, poets, actors etc it will be the audience who will provide realization through adulation and fame and fortune by continually turning up in the audience and by buying the artist's work whatever that may be, for example, books, cds etc. then they have found themselves in the world of entertainment and the arts. **GC**

"For me life has been either
a wake or a wedding".

Actor Peter O'Toole

What is being implied here is that life is full of ups and downs especially for colorful people like O'Toole. You can be up one minute and down the next. Some people can be said to be perfectly balanced but life can be boring by the same token. In the world of entertainment there can be lots of opportunities there for the taking. Most artists tend to take them and the more reticent usually stay in the background and may be happily settled down with a young family. Mr. O'Toole apparently lived life to the full and was determined to enjoy the ride. The downside of the film business is that there is a lot of temptation around what with drugs, alcohol, and women to name three. Then when some actors or actresses get hooked on substances, they can go astray and find themselves in darker places and thus we have the wakes which Peter

O' Toole referred to as above. A perfect balance may suffice but often doesn't. **GC**

"Men of power have no time to read;
yet men who do not read
are unfit for power".
Michael *Foot* – Former Labour Leader.

What I understand here in relation to the above comment is that all men and women should read as reading is at the very essence of knowledge and an absence of reading does not bode well for people at all levels of society especially in the corridors of power.

It may be that those in power genuinely have little time to read but that they should put aside some precious time to do so otherwise they are literally cheating their audience because their lack of reading will come across even to people of moderate intelligence. It is often said that the brain dies if it is not fed (Gore) and I think that this can be applied when the gifted art of reading is put aside or neglected by those in power. If debates in politics for example are conducted by people who are not reading constantly then the quality of such debates will be diminished drastically and suffer due to a famine of reading. **GC**

"Express yourself, so you
can respect yourself".
Madonna – Pop Singer.

"It's my rule never to lose me temper till it
would be detrimental to keep it".
Playwright – Sean O'Casey.

"There is nothing to writing.
All you have to do is sit at a
typewriter and open a vein".
American *Sportswriter* – Walter 'Red' Smith.

"It is easier to love humanity as a whole
than to love one's neighbor."
Philosopher - Eric Hoffer.

You can't control the length of your life
but you can control its width and depth".
Writer – Tom Anderson.

Everyone knows that they are going to die someday. Yet they do not know when this will take place or at what age. Most people undergo birth, puberty, maturity and old age. However, some people die young. This can happen for a number of reasons, including terminal illness or a fatal car crash.

I think what the writer is saying here is that you can look after your health and enjoy yourself into the bargain. He means that you can still have a good time without punishing your body but that the emphasis is on being happy whilst being careful because you are only here once. Therefore it is essential that you embrace common sense without compromising your health. This is what he means perhaps when he uses the yardstick of width and depth. **GC**

"When you are down and out something always turns up – and it is usually the noses of your friends".
Orson Welles – Actor/Director.

"Choose a job you love and you will never have to work a day in your life".
Chinese Philosopher – Confucius.

"There is no formula for success, but there is a formula for failure and that is to try to please everybody".
Rebel Without A Cause Director – Nicholas Ray.

"Hearing Elvis for the first time
was like bursting out of jail".
Singer/Songwriter – *Bob* Dylan.

"The opera ain't over till the fat lady sings.
U.S. Basketball Coach – Dick Motta.

"All charming people have
something to conceal.
Usually their total dependence on
the appreciation of others!"
Critic/Journalist – Cyril Connolly.

I suppose that when all is said and done, charming people have a certain void in their lives otherwise they wouldn't act as they do, although charm is persuasive and very attractive when used well.

I would guess that like most if not all actors they do rely on the appreciation of others. If that appreciation is not forthcoming, then I would imagine that they go back into their cave to lick their wounds. When they eventually emerge from their caves, refreshed and rearing to go, they go back to what they do best and that is to charm their friends and their audience. **(GC)**

Note....

A selection of verse from W.B. Yeats
(1865-1939)

When you are old and grey and full of sleep,
And nodding by the fire,
take down this book
And slowly read and dream of the soft look
Your eyes once had and of
their shadows deep.

(When you are old) (1893)

Though leaves are many, the root is one;
Through all the lying days of my youth,
I swayed my leaves and flowers in the sun;
Now I may wither into the truth.

(The coming of wisdom with Time) (1914)

Fifteen apparitions have I seen;
The worst a coat upon a coat-hanger.

(The Apparitions) (1939)

Now that my ladders gone
I must lie down where all ladders start
In the foul rag and bone shop of the heart.

(The Circus Animals Desertion) (1939) Part 3.

Think like a wise man, but express
yourself like the common people.
(1935)

In dreams begins responsibility.
(1914)

We make out of the quarrel with others,
rhetoric, but out of the quarrel
with ourselves, poetry.
(1924)

When I was young,
I had not given a penny for a song
Did not the poet sing it with such airs,
That one believed he had a sword upstairs.

(All Things can tempt me) (1910)

She bid me take life easy, as the
grass grows on the weirs;
But I was young and foolish,
and now am full of tears.
(Down by the Salley Gardens) (1889)

The light of evening, Lissadell,
Great windows open to the south,

Two girls in silk kimonos, both
Beautiful, one a gazelle.
(In memory of Eva Gore Booth
and Con Markiewicz) (1933)

Land of Hearts Desire,
Where beauty has no ebb, decoy no flood,
But joy is wisdom, Time an endless song.
(The land of Hearts Desire) (1894)

Like a long-legged fly upon the stream
His mind moves upon silence.
(Long-legged Fly) (1939)

Note.......

**An appropriate poem as an
inspiration to the
overall theme of the book is the following,
written by General *MacArthur*.**

CREDO

Youth is not a time of life;
it is a state of mind;
It is a temper of the will,
A quality of the imagination,
Vigor of the emotions,

A predominance of courage over timidity,
Of the appetite for adventure
over love of ease.

Nobody grows old merely by
living a number of years,
People grow old only by
deserting their ideals;
Years wrinkle the skin
But to give up enthusiasm
– wrinkles the soul.
Worry, doubt, self-distrust, fear and despair,
These are the long, long years
that bow the head
And turn the growing spirit back to dust.

Whether seventy or sixteen,
there is in every beings
Heart the love of wonder,
The sweet amazement of the stars
And the star-like things and thoughts
The undaunted challenge of events
The unfailing childlike
appetite for what next.
And the joy and the game of life.

You are as young as your faith,
as old as your doubt,
As young as your self-confidence,

As old as your fear;
As young as your hope,
As old as your despair.

So long as your heart receives
messages of beauty,
Cheer, courage, grandeur and power
From the earth, from man, from the infinite,
So long you are young.

When the wires are all down
And all the control place of your heart
Is covered with the snow of pessimism
And the ice of cynicism,
Then you are old indeed
And may God have mercy on your soul.

PORTRAIT OF A GREAT ROMANTIC

JOHN KEATS (1795-1821)

In his short life, which spanned only some 26 years, John Keats became immortalized as one of a select band of English Romantic poets.

His contemporaries included Blake, Coleridge, Wordsworth, Shelley and Byron, all of very different backgrounds and expertise.

The word has it that they actually disliked each other to an extreme. Keats once said of Bryon – *"Now speak of Lord Byron and me. There is this difference between us. He describes what he sees. I describe what I imagine. Mine is the hardest task".* What the English Romantic poets did share and believe in was that of the mission of the poet. In Germany and later on in France, celebrated writers like Chateaubriand, Hugo and De Vigry were very much influenced and motivated by English poets of the Romantic era. Most were of the belief that in a subtle way, the imagination was institutionalized by the emergence of the poetical craft of the poet as an unique, mystical individual, who was said to possess a special, alluring faculty which distinguished him from his fellow men.

Keats was born in London, the eldest of 4 children, 3 boys and a girl. Educated at Enfield, he showed great prowess at sport, notably excelling in cricket and boxing. At that stage, he displayed little, if any interest in literacy. In his final 2 years at Enfield, he became a voracious reader, having a penchant for Greek Mythology.

As 1810 came to a close, Keats began an apprenticeship to a surgeon – apothecary in Enfield and thus left school. However, he continued a friendship with Cowden-Clarke, the headmaster's son at Enfield. Cowden-Clarke saw great promise in him and encouraged him to pursue his literary talents. He wrote his first poem in 1814 entitled *"Lines in Imitation of Spenser"*. After a row with his master, Keats went to London to live and became a student at Guys Hospital. During 1815, he wrote a number of notable odes, including *"To Hope"*, *"To Apollo"* and three sonnets on the subject of woman.

Around the same year he began to read Wordsworth's poetry. Heavily influenced by Wordsworth's work, Keats wrote *"O Solitude"*, which was published in the liberal journal *"The Examiner"*. His friend, Cowden-Clarke introduced him to Leigh Hunt, the editor of the Examiner. Hunt took Keats under his wing and provided literary contacts for him through people such as John Hamilton Reynolds and the renowned painter Benjamin Haydon. During that time he also met Percy Shelley, a celebrated Romantic poet. The meeting was not conducive as Keats was wary of Shelley, being older and wiser and at that time there seemed to be a love/hate relationship between poets of that genre. In November 1816, Keats famous sonnet **"On first looking into Chapman's Homer",** was published in the Examiner. The same year seen the publication of **"I stood Tip-Toe Upon a Little Hill"** and **"Sleep and Poetry"** in addition to a selection of other work including rhymed epistles and miscellaneous poems. His first volume of poetry, entitled **"Poems",** was published in 1817, but apart from adulation from his friends, the book was not a success due to adverse criticism and reviews.

During 1817, Keats spent some time away from London. Two of his favourite *'getaways'* were the Isle of Wight and Margate, where he spent a lot of time in the company of his brother Tom. When summer arrived, he visited his friend Bailey in Oxford. It was around this period that he decided to use some of his personal letters as a vehicle in forming expressions on his thoughts of love, philosophy, poetry and of his experience of the people and events surrounding his general life. His letters have been noted by critics for their wit, vivacity and profound intelligence and have been regarded as equally important as some of his renowned verse. The letters were published to high acclaim in 1848 and again in 1878.

In November 1817, Keats completed, what some believe to be, his most ambitious project that of Endymion. In December he read some passages of it to Wordsworth who rebuked him by referring to it as a *'pretty piece of paganism'.*

Attending Hazlitts lectures on English poetry greatly improved Keats poetical technique and he was fast maturing as a classical poet. By this time his brother Tom was dying with tuberculosis. Keats dedicated a lot of his time to nursing Tom. In June, his brother George married and immigrated to America. Keats, and his friend Brown, spent the summer touring the Lake District, Scotland and Northern Ireland. Influenced greatly by the scenery, some of it is reflected in passages of Hyperion. During his stay in the West Highlands, Keats contracted a throat infection from which he would never fully recover. On his return to London, he resumed nursing Tom. Things began to get too much for Keats, for as well as the imminent death of Tom and George's emigration, he became somewhat disillusioned with poetry.

Nevertheless, he vowed to carry on and remarked to Tom, that after his own death, he would still be among the Great English Poets. After Tom died in December, Keats moved to Hampstead near to where Fanny Brown lived and with whom he fell madly in love with. The relationship was not to bring him lasting happiness due to a lack of means and a morbid preoccupation with his own impending illness.

In 1818-19 Keats had his best year in terms of poetical excellence, development and productivity. Comparable to Shelley's golden period in Italy around the same time, Keats worked feverishly on Hyperion, The Eve of St. Agnes and The Eve of St Mark, whilst in Sussex. When he arrived back in Hampstead in early February, for a while he relented, but again between March and May he excelled in writing some of the odes of which he is famous for amongst great collections of Great English poets. In succession he composed *"On a Grecian Urn", "To Pysche", "To a Nightingale"* and *"On Melancholy"*, as well as the Sonnets *"Fame"* and *"Why Did I Laugh Tonight?"*.

In late 1819, *"Ode to Autumn"* and a second version of Hyperion, entitled *"The Fall of Hyperion"* followed.

Unfortunately, in comparison with his great resurgence, his unhappy love life and financial state left him ill and dejected, almost to the point of despair. On a visit from America, George was shocked to find him in such poor spirits. Keats began the unfinished *"Cap and Bells"* but in February 1820, he became seriously ill with tuberculosis and was rapidly fading away. He did manage to get his second volume of poems published, but shortly afterwards became too weak to write. The reviewers this time were generous in their praise of his second volume of poems.

However, this was secondary to his health condition, which drastically worsened. Keats was nursed by the Hunts and then by Fanny Brown and her Mother. He then put his affairs in order and sailed for Italy with his friend the painter Joseph Severn in September 1820. He refused Shelley's kind offer to join him at Pisa, went to Rome instead and died the following February.

Keats reputation as a great poet continued to grow during the 19th century and his admirers included Tennyson, Matthew Arnold and the Pre-Raphaelites. In the 20th century and to this day, he together with Wordsworth, are perhaps the best known and widely read of all the English Romantic Poets. His odes such as *"To Autumn"* and *"On a Grecian Urn"* are as popular as anything written by Shakespeare. Who knows just what he may have accomplished had he lived longer!

FAMOUS ODES FROM JOHN KEATS
1795 – 1821

ODE TO A NIGHTINGALE

My heart aches, and a drowsy
numbness pains
My sense, as though of hemlock I had drunk,
Or emptied some dull opiate to the drains
One minute past, and Lethe-
wards had sunk:
Tis not through envy of thy happy lot,
But being too happy in thine happiness, -
That thou, light-winged Dryad of the trees,
In some melodious plot
Of beechen green, and
shadows numberless,
Singest of summer in full-throated ease.

O, for a draught of vintage! that hath been
Cool'd a long age in the deep-delved earth,
Tasting of Flora and the country green,
Dance, and Provencal song,
and sunburnt mirth!
O for a beaker full of the warm South,
Full of the true, the blushful Hippocrene,
With beaded bubbles winking at the brim,
And purple-stained mouth;
That I might drink, and leave
the world unseen,
And with thee fade away
into the forest dim:

Fade far away, dissolve, and quite forget
What thou among the leaves
hast never known,
The weariness, the ever, and the fret
Here, where men sit and hear
each other groan;
Where palsy shakes a few,
sad, last gray hairs,
Where youth grows pale, and
spectre-thin, and dies;
Where but to think is to be full of sorrow
And leaden-eyed despairs,
Where Beauty cannot keep
her lustrous eyes,

Or new Love pine at them
beyond to-morrow.

Away! Away! For I will fly to thee,
Not charioted by Bacchus and his pards,
But on the viewless wings of Poesy,
Though the dull brain perplexes and retards;
Already with thee! tender is the night,
And haply the Queen-Moon is on her throne,
Cluster'd around by all her starry Fays;
But here there is no light,
Save what from heaven is
with the breezes blown
Through verdurous glooms
and winding mossy ways.

I cannot see what flowers are at my feet,
Nor what soft incense hangs
upon the boughs,
But, in embalmed darkness,
guess each sweet
Wherewith the seasonable month endows
The grass, the thicket, and
the fruit-tree wild;
White hawthorn, and the pastoral eglantine;
Fast fading violets cover'd up in leaves;
And mid-May's eldest child,
The coming musk-rose, full of dewy wine,

the murmurous haunt of
flies on summer eves.

Darkling I listen; and, for many a time
I have been half in love with easeful Death,
Call'd him soft names in
many a mused thyme,
To take into the air my quiet breath;
Now more than ever seems it rich to die,
To cease upon the midnight with no pain,
While thou art pouring forth thy soul abroad
In such an ecstasy!
Still wouldst thou sing, and
I have ears in vain-
To thy high requiem become a sod.

Thou wast not born for
death, immortal Bird!
No hungry generations tread thee down;
The voice I hear this passing night was heard
In ancient days by emperor and clown:
Perhaps the self-same song
that found a path
Through the sad heart of Ruth,
when, sick for home,
She stood in tears amid the alien corn;
The same that oft-times hath
Charm'd magic casements,
opening on the foam

Of perilous seas, in faery lands forlorn.

Forlorn! The very word is like a bell
To toll me back from thee to my sole self!
Adieu! the fancy cannot cheat so well
As she is fam'd to do, deceiving elf.
Adieu! adieu! thy plaintive anthem fades
Past the near meadows,
over the still stream,
Up the hill-side; and now 'tis buried deep
In the next valley-glades;
Was it a vision, or a waking dream?
Fled is that music: - Do I wake or sleep?

ODE ON A GRECIAN URN

Thou still unravish'd bride of quietness,
Thou foster-child of silence and slow time,
Sylvan historian, who canst thus express
A flowery tale more sweetly
than our rhyme;
What leaf-fring'd legend
haunts about thy shape?
Of deities or mortals, or of both,
In Tempe or the dales of Arcady?
What men or gods are these?
What maidens loth?

What mad pursuit? What
struggle to escape?
What pipes and timbrels? What wild ecstasy?

Heard melodies are sweet,
but those unheard
Are sweeter; therefore, ye
soft pipes, play on;
Not to the sensual ear, but, more endear'd
Pipe to the spirit ditties of no tone:
Fair youth, beneath the trees,
thou canst not leave
Thy song, nor ever can those trees be bare;
Bold Lover, never, never canst thou kiss,
Though winning near the goal
– yet, do not grieve;
She cannot fade, though
thou hast not thy bliss,
For ever wilt thou love, and she be fair!

Ah, happy, happy boughs! that cannot shed
Your leaves, nor ever bid the Spring adieu;
And, happy melodist, unwearied,
For ever piping songs for ever new;
More happy love! more happy, happy love!
For ever warm and still to be enjoy'd,
For ever panting, and for ever young.
All breathing human passion far above.

That leaves a heart high-
sorrowful and cloy'd,
A burning forehead, and a parching tongue.

Who are these coming to the sacrifice?
To what green altar, O mysterious priest,
Lead'st thou that heifer lowing at the skies,
And all her silken flanks with garlands drest?
What little town by river or sea shore,
Or mountain-built with peaceful citadel,
Is emptied of this folk, this pious morn?
And, little town, thy streets for evermore
Will silent be; and not a soul to tell
Why thou are desolate, can e'er return.

O Attic shape! Fair attitude! with brede
Of marble men and maidens overwrought,
With forest branches and the trodden weed;
Thou, silent form, dost tease
us out of thought
As doth eternity: Cold Pastoral!
When old age shall this generation waste,
Thou shalt remain, in midst of other woe
Than ours, a friend to man,
to whom thou say'st,
"Beauty is truth, truth beauty," – that is all
Ye know on earth, and all ye need to know.

ODE ON MELANCHOLY

No, no, go not to Lethe, neither twist
Wolf's-bane, tight-rooted,
for its poisonous wine;
Nor suffer thy pale forehead to be kissed
By nightshade, ruby grape of Prosperpine;
Make not your rosary of yew-berries,
Nor let the beetle, nor the death-moth be
Your mournful Psyche, nor the downy owl
A partner in your sorrow's mysteries;
For shade to shade will come too drowsily,
And drown the wakeful anguish of the soul.

But when the melancholy fit shall fall
Sudden from heaven like a weeping cloud,
That fosters the droop-headed flowers all,
And hides the green hill in an April shroud;
Then glut thy sorrow on a morning rose,
Or on the rainbow of the salt sand-wave,
Or on the wealth of globed peonies;
Or if thy mistress some rich anger shows,
Emprison her soft hand, and let her rave,
And feed deep, deep upon
her peerless eyes.

She dwells with Beauty-
Beauty that must die;
And Joy, whose hand is ever at his lips

Bidding adieu; and aching Pleasure nigh,
Turning to Poison while the bee-mouth sips:
Ay, in the very temple of delight
Veil'd Melancholy has her sovran shrine,
Though seen of none save him
whose strenuous tongue
Can burst Joy's grape against his palate fine;
His soul shall taste the sadness of her might,
And be among her cloudy trophies hung.

TO AUTUMN

Season of mists and mellow fruitfulness,
Close bosom-friend of the maturing sun;
Conspiring with him how to load and bless
With fruit the vines that round
the thatch-eves run;
To bend with apples the
moss'd cottage-trees,
And fill all fruit with ripeness to the core;
To swell the gourd, and
plump the hazel shells
With a sweet kernel; to set budding more,
And still more, later flowers for the bees,
Until they think warm days will never cease,
For summer has o'er-brimm'd
their clammy cells.

Who hath not seen thee oft amid thy store?
Sometimes whoever seeks abroad may find
Thee sitting careless on a granary floor,
Thy hair soft-lifted by the winnowing wind;
Or on a half-reap'd furrow sound asleep,
Drows'd with the fume of
poppies, while thy hook
Spares the next swath and
all its twined flowers:

And sometimes like a gleaner
thou dost keep
Steady thy laden head across a brook;
Or by a cyder-press, with patient look,
Thou watchest the last
oozing hours by hours.

Where are the songs of Spring?
Ay, where are they?
Think not of them, thou hast thy music too,-
While barred clouds bloom
the soft-dying day,
And touch the stubble-plains with rosy hue;
Then in a wailful choir the
small gnats mourn
Among the river sallows, borne aloft
Or sinking as the light wind lives or dies;
And full-grown lambs loud
bleat from hilly bourn:

Hedge-crickets sing; and
now with treble soft
The red-breast whistles from a garden-croft;
And gathering swallows twitter in the skies.

Notes.....

Great Minds Think Alike!

The impressive three-story Georgian style terrace block in Church Place in Lurgan was the residence of successive generations of the Donnelly/O'Neill/Deeny families. In recent years, Dr. Donnell Deeny had his practice in rooms on the ground floor, until new premises were built in Hill Street.

Arthur Donnelly constructed the building in 1885 and it stands as a great testament to 19th century architecture. Arthur Donnelly to this day has great- great- grandchildren and 'Great minds think alike' and that saying could be applied to the dynasty of Messrs. Donnelly / O'Neill and Deeny in business and professional circles!

THE BIG CHURCH

The main focal point of Lurgan would probably be Christ Church, affectionately referred to as *'The Big Church'.* A truly outstanding work of gothic architecture, it is situated in the Centre of town and is thee landmark of Lurgan Town.

The church was consecrated in May 1863 and serves the Church of Ireland community in the parish of Shankill.

When a new visitor drives into Lurgan, the first sight they invariably see is 'the Big Church' with its impressive spire and four-sided town clock. In every respect of the word, 'the Big Church' has earned the title of Thee landmark of Lurgan

A BUSINESS THAT BORE FRUIT!

Probably the most popular fruit and vegetable shop in the town, Kelly's was a bustling hive of industry that never seemed to slacken. With their impressive display outside and busy interior, Kelly's was second to none.

Opened in 1930 or thereabouts, Kelly's enjoyed a thriving trade until recent times when it finally closed. A business that literally came to fruition!

THE CHAPEL

A fine, impressive Church of splendid architecture. Built in 1833 on land at North Street, donated by the Brownlow Family, St. Peter's is renowned for its beauty, both interior and exterior and contains splendid marbling effects inside the Church.

Major works were carried out in 1927 involving the Italian Sculptor, Signor Mommassi . A stately building that serves the people well.

TO THE SCHOOL ON THE HILL

St. Michael's Grammar School at Cornakinnegar Road in Lurgan was originally an all - girls boarding school. St, Michaels now caters for both sexes and is part of a blueprint where various schools in the Lurgan area will be transformed into one huge building that will facilitate all modes of learning. The old building seen many eminent scholars emerge from the gates of St. Michaels who were at the forefront of teaching and business in the area.

ARE YA GOING TO THE 'FLICKS'?

In its heyday, the old Lyric Cinema was the place to be! During the 50's and 60's especially. Crowds were streaming onto the street, the venue was that popular. Before the advent of the video, the massive wide screen adorned with vivid Technicolor was a sight to behold. Audiences got the feeling that they were being transported to a new dimension. Many a relationship that resulted in marriage was initiated in the stalls or 'flea-pit' of the Lyric Cinema!

'Coorting' was plentiful amid the velvety tones of Elvis Presley and the bravado of John Wayne. No need for ecstasy or artificial substances! 'Dough' went a long way as a 'quid' got you a seat in the Lyric, a fish-supper on the way home and still loose change in yer pocket! Oh happy days!

'Coorting' meant Courting

THE COLLEGE, THE SCHOOL
WITH A RENOWNED PAST!

One of Lurgan's architectural gems with a landscape to match is Lurgan College, situated just off the Lough Road. The original buildings date back to 1873, and although modernity has altered it somewhat, it still retains much of its classical design. The accepted father founder of the School was Samuel Watts (1787-1850).

When Samuel Watts passed away in 1850, his estate totaled almost £10,000. Calculated into today's currency, that would be a tidy sum of around £2 million!

A COSY RESIDENCE FOR THE
OLD FOLK!

The Old Manor House (now demolished) has been a sanctuary and a center for a bit of 'craic' since 1948 for old folk. Many a joke and fine banter was heard in the hallowed surroundings of the 'Manor House'. Originally a residence for Lord Lurgan's land-steward John Hancock, the County Welfare Committee bought it off its last private owner, a W.W. Bassett, a surgeon in-charge at Lurgan Hospital in 1948. It remained an old folks home until in recent years, the Health & Social Services Board decided to pull the curtain on the Manor.

It was demolished to make way for a new modern complex of sheltered dwellings called Manor Court.

FAMILIAR EXPRESSIONS EXPLAINED

SOUR GRAPES - Results when we have failed to achieve successfully what we have set out to do. This usually puts us in a foul mood and we invariably end up belittling everything and everyone.

The term Sour Grapes, goes back to a scene in Aesop's fable about a fox that was unable to reach the succulent grapes in a vineyard, trails away muttering, *"I see they are sour anyway!"*

KEEP DANGER AT BAY - In times of trouble or conflict we often are heard to say - 'Try and keep danger at bay.' This particular expression dates back to the beliefs of the Greeks and Romans that the Bay Laurel tree provided protection from bolts of lightning. Therefore they thought that by wearing bay leaves on their heads, they would be safe. During the Great Plague of London in 1655, people unwisely thought that wearing bay leaves would make them immune to the plaque. As 80,000 people perished, sadly their optimism was ill-founded.

NAKED TRUTH - If someone is giving an account of something, for example a disaster or a business venture and they leave nothing out in their description, they could be said to be giving you the Naked Truth. This one goes back to an old fable concerning Truth and Falsehood who went for a swim together. Falsehood got out of the water first and put on Truth's clothing. Truth could not bring himself to wear Falsehood's clothing and he walked away naked. The moral of the story is Truth with- out any of Falsehoods covering is the *"Naked Truth!"*

SHIP-SHAPE AND BRISTOL FASHION - This goes back to the days of the sailing ships. As the safety and well-being of passengers and crew was paramount, it was essential to check that everything on board was in first-class condition and functioning to a high degree before a long voyage was embarked on.

Bristol Port at that time was considered to be an excellent and ultra-efficient port. So the phrase given to a ship as '*Ship-Shape and Bristol Fashion*' was coined.

Today, anything that is well-organised, neat and tidy and in excellent condition is awarded the accolade!

RED-HERRINGS - A phrase used to deflect or mislead someone, or to put them off your tracks. Often used as a ploy in detective novels. Apparently it dates back to the training of hounds in fox-hunting. If herrings were laid across the hound's path, the scent of them would deflect and mislead the hounds away from the proper trail.

FEELING UNDER THE WEATHER?

✗ When the alarm clock goes off, the best part of the day is over.

🖊 Hot words never resulted in cool judgement.

🖊 Many people never learn to relax. Others never learn anything else.

🖊 The man who always loses his head probably has a screw loose.

🖊 Lots of people don't get ulcers, they just infect other people.

🖊 Are you aware of the many mistakes you'd make if you didn't sleep a third of the day?

🖊 Contentment often means you are too lazy to kick up a fuss.

🖊 The greatest enemy of the human soul is a guilty conscience.

🖊 There's not a worry in the world worth the worry.

🖊 Even a waiter finally comes to those who wait.

🖊 We rarely weather the storm by storming the weather.

✗ It takes a worried man to sing a worried song.

✗ Better April showers than the breath of the ocean in gold.

✗ Wind from the East is neither good for man or beast.

✗ A Kerry shower lasts 24 hours...

✗ The losing horse blames the saddle.

✗ Men with clenched fists cannot shake hands.

✗ An angry man is seldom reasonable:
A reasonable man is seldom angry.

✗ The less said, the easiest mended.

✗ The dark is light enough.

✗ The best way to get rid of a hot-head is to give him the cold shoulder.

✗ Float like a butterfly, sting like a bee.

(Mohammad Ali - Boxer)

Gerry Casey

✒ Houston Tranquility Base here.
The Eagle has landed -
'Buzz' Aldrin - American Astronaut

(Second man on the moon)

✒ What's the use of worrying?
It never was worth- while.
So pack up your troubles in your old Kit-bag.
and smile, smile, smile.

'Pack Up Your Troubles' (1915 song)
by George Asaf (1880-1951)
British Song-writer.

✒ A man's conscience tells him what he
shouldn't do, but it doesn't keep him from
doing it.

✒ Many of us won't be content with our lot
in life until it's a lot more.

✒ God makes a promise, faith believes it, hope
anticipates it, patience quietly awaits it.

✒ People who fly into a rage always make a
bad landing.

✗ The happiest people are those too busy to wonder if they are.

✗ Patience is the art of concealing your impatience.

✗ Laugh with people - not at them!

✗ The trouble with people nowadays is that they want to get to the top without starting at the bottom.

✗ No pain - No gain!

✗ Patience is a quality most needed when exhausted.

✗ Better to be patient on the road than in hospital.

✗ Anger is like a fire extinguisher. It should only be used in an emergency!

✗ The best tranquilizer is a good conscience.

✗ You are not a dynamic person just because you blow your top!

↗ Anger is a wind that blows out a candle in the dark.

↗ The emptier the pot, the quicker the boil.

↗ Everybody wants to change everything in the world, except themselves.

↗ What a married couple should save for old age is themselves.

↗ Blessed is the person, whose too busy to worry in the day time and too full of sleep to worry at night.

↗ Sleep comes easy with a clear conscience.

↗ If we are not contented in ourselves, stop searching for it elsewhere.

↗ Blowing your stack causes air pollution.

↗ Control your anger, don't let if control you.

↗ Nothing worthwhile happens in a hurry - be patient!

↗ A peace above all earthly dignities.
A still and quiet conscience.

(Shakespeare)

✗ Ah! when shall all men's good
Be each man's rule and universal peace
Lie like a shaft of light across the land?

(The Golden Year 1846 - Tennyson)

✗ Drive carefully! If motorists give more ground there'd be fewer in it!

A SELECTION OF JOKES AND WITTICISMS FROM HOME AND FURTHER AFIELD

HEAVY HANDED

A pet owner took his Great Dane to the vet. *"I hope you can help,"* he said. *"There seems to be something wrong with his eyes."* The vet picked the huge dog up and stared into his eyes. *"I'm afraid I'll have to put him down,"* said the vet, almost out of breath.

The owner looked sad, *"Why?"* he spluttered. *"Because he's too heavy for me,"* smiled the vet.

WORTH THEIR WEIGHT

A man goes into a shop and asks for a pound of spuds. *"They're kilos now,"* says the man in the shop. *"That's alright,"* says the man, *"I'll have a pound of kilos instead."*

OUT AT NIGHT FOR A BITE

A male mosquito walks out of cinema with his girlfriend one night. He looks lovingly into her eyes and says, *"Fancy a bite then love!"*

What do you call an Italian with a rubber toe? Roberto!!
PORRIDGE - NOT CEREAL

Into the prison arrived a new convict. Gigantic, evil-looking, a nasty piece of work, made Hannibal Lector look like a choir boy. None of the other inmates knew what his crime was.

During breakfast one cold, icy morning, a pale nervous inmate told his pals, *"Ye know,"* he gulped, *"He's a serial killer!"*

Recoiling in traumatic fear, they shrieked, "How da ye know?" "Well," he said, "Early one morning I heard him growl - 'I could murder a bowl of cornflakes!'"

HUSH PUPPY!

Did ye hear about the dog that loves garlic? - His bark is worse than his bite!

A CRAFTY CHOP

A character went into a local butchers, and said to the assistant, "I'll bet ye a tenner ye can't reach them two cuts of meat up there!" "Well I can't," shouted back the assistant, "the steaks are too high!"

Jimmy - *"What's the difference between ignorance and apathy?"*

Barry - *"I haven't a clue and I don't give a damn!"*

Two flies on a teapot had a bit of a barney.
It all started when one of them
flew off the handle!

TOO MUCH OF A GOOD THING!

Awful sad news has been reported today. Police have found an ice-cream man stone dead in his van. When the coroner examined the body, it was covered in chocolate sauce, raspberry ripple, and with a helping of crushed nuts. The verdict was that he had topped himself!

PRINCE CHARMING

A fella walks into a bar and asks the barman if he'll give him a free drink if he shows him something out of this world.

The barman says, *"Okay."*

The fella pulls out a hamster, which starts dancing and singing, 'It's not unusual' a hit for Tom Jones.

"God, that's powerful," says the barman and gives the fella a free drink.

"If I show you something else outta this world, will ye give me another free drink?"

"I will indeed," *says the barman* "You're some pup!"

This time, the fella pulls out a tiny piano, a hamster and a wee frog. The hamster starts playing the piano, the wee frog dances and sings, *'Life's a Roller Coaster'* a hit for wee Ronan Keating. The barman, by this time completely spellbound, quickly gives the fella another drink on the house. Quietly watching everything in a corner, a man in a pin-stripe suit casually steps forward, *"I'd like to buy your wee frog. Name your price, any price!"*

The fella nods and names a price, *"Are you crazy?"* says the barman to the fella, *"You could make a fortune out of that wee frog!"*

"Say nothing!" *says the fella,* "The hamsters a ventriloquist!"

You Can't Get Better Than This

There's a quaint little saying,
if practiced each day,
Would change the whole world,
in a wonderful way,
And this little saying if practiced by all,

From the young to the old and
the great to the small
Would make life seem brighter,
would give us all hope.
When we're finding it hard
with troubles to cope.
It's counting your blessings,
taking pleasure in gifts,
And it's simple; you **'Cannot
get better than this.'**

The scent of the sheets taken in off the line,
The taste of the grape in the glass of wine,
The sun on your face, when
the clouds disappear,
And the joy and excitement
when Christmas draws near.
The sight of spring flowers,
when winter is gone,
The depth of the ocean the sky sits upon,
Cold toes by the fireside, isn't it bliss?
You simply **'Cannot get better than this.'**

A long drink of water when
parched by the thirst,
On hearing your daughter in
her spellings came first.
A cool hand on hot foreheads,
when fevers are high,

The sound of a newborn, when
he first starts to cry.
The first day of the holidays,
when schooldays are over,
Having a picnic in a field full of clover.
Catching the bus, you were
sure that you'd miss,
You simply **'Cannot get better than this.'**

The smell of home baking, the
taste of fresh bread,
The soft feel of your pillow,
when you fall into bed.
The strength of a friendship, that
lasts through the years,
And those who stick by you
through laughter and tears.
The color of twilight before it gets dark,
Watching the toddlers on
swings in the park.
Hugging your children as
they give you a kiss,
You simply **'Cannot get better than this.'**

Resting tired limbs in a bath full of bubbles,
Helping a friend to cope with her troubles,
Finding the car keys you'd
thought lost forever,

Passing exams when you
thought you weren't clever!
Learning to drive and then passing the test,
Watching the sun setting over the West.
Why be unhappy, there's too much to miss
'Cos you simply **'Cannot get better than this.'**

So this little saying, old
fashioned, appealing,
Is really worth saying, when
it's sad you are feeling.
There could not be a more simple
and homespun approach.
As the troubles of living
continually encroach.
Think of this saying and quote it in earnest.
When its 'out of the frying pan
and into the furnace,'
And I guarantee soon things
will not be amiss,
For you simply just **'Cannot
get better than this.'**

Beautiful Snow...

by Joseph Warren Watson

There is a certain mystique and a twist in the tale surrounding the composition of this beautiful autobiographical account.

On a cold wintry night in Cincinnati, Ohio, in the early 1860s, the body of a young girl of twenty-three was found lying near the Commercial Hotel. The young girl was idolized by her parents, but sadly had fallen into bad company and now had met her demise in unsavory circumstances.

The author of the poem, a Joseph Warren Watson, who coincidentally died also at twenty-three, was moved by the young woman's tragic tale and consequently composed the poem in her memory. He himself died in 1872.

Apparently, Joseph was a young man of immense literary talent and had written some fine poems. **'Beautiful Snow'** was one of his finest and in fact world renowned in literacy circles. It was said at the time that he was always profoundly conscious of his imminent young death and sure enough he fell to the prevalent fatal illness of those times, the dreaded consumption.

Watson's poem achieved a certain popularity and warmth. However, when it was discovered found in a scrapbook of a man of seventy-two, who had just died, it more or less entered the 'Hall of Fame' as it transpired that the man with the scrapbook was indeed the man who had originally found the poor girl lying in the street on that cold wintry night in Cincinnati.

I suppose that there is a reason for everything and for life itself. For destiny to work out so poignantly encapsulates the mystery of life and the stories both internally and externally which are constantly weaving the final chapters of demise which present themselves to each and every one of us as individuals on the planet.

It could be that some of us are given precursors or signs of our fate and destiny either consciously or subconscious. We may not recognize them as clear cut as Joseph did.

Coincidences can provide us with certain comforts when we attempt to unravel such mysteries as that described above. The very fact that the young girl was twenty three when she died and that Joseph shared the same age and further, that the man with the scrapbook originally found the girl in the street speaks volumes for the great story and poem that was to emanate from it.

Can you the reader report any coincidences that have made you wonder on how little we really know about life and the meaning of it?

Note......

Beautiful Snow

Oh, the snow, the beautiful snow,
Filling the sky and the earth below,
Over the housetops, over the street,
Over the heads of the people you meet,
Dancing, flirting, skimming along,
Beautiful snow, it can do nothing wrong;
Flying to kiss a fair lady's cheek,
Clinging to lips in a frolic-some freak,
Beautiful snow from heaven above,
Pure as an angel, gentle as love.

Oh, the snow, the beautiful snow,
How the flakes gather and laugh as they go,
Whirling about in maddening fun,
Chasing, laughing, hurrying by,
It lights on the face,
And it sparkles the eye,

And the dogs with a bark and a bound
Snap at the crystals as they eddy around.
The town is alive.
And its heart is aglow
To welcome the coming of
the beautiful snow.

How wildly the crowd goes swaying along,
Hailing each other with humor and song!
How the gay sledges like meteors flash by,
Bright for a moment,
Then lost to the eye,
Ringing, swinging, dashing they go
Over the crest of the beautiful snow,
Snow so pure as it falls from the sky,
To be trampled in time by
the crowds rushing by,
To be trampled and tracked by
the thousands of feet,
Till it blends with the filth in
the horrible street.

Once I was pure as the snow but I fell,
Fell like the snowflakes from heaven to hell,
Fell to be trampled as filth in the street,
Fell to be scoffed at,
To be spat at and beat,
Pleading, cursing, and dreading to die,
Selling my soul to whoever would buy,

Dealing in shame for a morsel of bread
Hating the living and fearing the dead.
Merciful God have I fallen so low?
And yet I was once
Like the beautiful snow.

Once I was fair like the beautiful snow,
With an eye like a crystal,
A heart like its glow.
Once I was loved for my innocent grace,
Flattered and sought for the
charms of my face.
Father, mother, sister and all,
God and myself, I have lost by my fall.
The vilest wretch that goes shivering by
Will make a wide sweep
Lest I wander too nigh,
For all that is on or above me I know,
There is nothing as pure as
the beautiful snow.

How strange it should be
That this beautiful snow
Should fall on a sinner
With nowhere to go!
How strange it should be,
When night comes again,
If the snow and the ice
Struck my desperate brain!

Fainting, freezing, dying alone,
Too wicked for prayer,
Too weak for a moan.
To be heard in the street
Of this crazy town
Gone mad in the joy of the
snow coming down,
To lie and to die in my terrible woe,
With a bed and a shroud
Of the beautiful snow.

Helpless and foul as the trampled snow,
Sinner, despair not,
Christ stoopeth low
To rescue the soul that is lost in sin
And raise it to life
And enjoyment again,
Groaning, bleeding, dying for thee,
The crucified hung on the accursed tree.
His accents of mercy
Fall soft on thine ear,
Is there mercy for me?
Will He heed my weak prayer?
O God, in the stream
That for sinners doth flow,
Wash me, and I shall be whiter than snow.
NEW WAYS
FOR NEW IDEAS

From the hayloft, a horse looks like a violin.
- Lord Chesterfield

A hen is only an eggs way of
making another egg.
- Samuel Butler

MAN - A creature made at the end of
the weeks work when God was tired.
- Mark Twain
My uncle is a Southern Planter. He's
an undertaker in Alabama.
- Fred Allen
ZOO - An excellent place to study the
habits of human beings. (Evan Esar)
-

XEROX - A trademark for a photocopying
device that can make rapid reproductions of
human error, perfectly.(Meele I. Meachan)
-

Genius in truth means little more
than the faculty of perceiving in an
un habitual way (William James).

Available.
I tried to tell them I was available,
Yet no-one called,
That I was friendly, kind and sociable,

Yet no one called,
To not listen to gossip and family rivalry,
Yet no one called,
If you're nasty, cruel and vindictive,
Do people call?
Up to no good planning
plotting and spiteful,
Do people call?
Do people feel intimidated or inferior?
Is that why they don't call?
If I was rich and had money in abundance,
I suppose every-one would call,
Irrespective of my personality or way
If that's the case, then I'm
glad that no-one calls!

Gerry Casey

IF YER IRISH
IRISH BLESSINGS

May there always be work
for your hands to do,
May your purse always hold a coin or two
May the sun always shine warm
on your windowpane
May a rainbow be certain to follow each rain
May the hand of a friend always be near you

*And may God fill your heart with
gladness to cheer you!*

May the Blessings of each day
Be the Blessings you need most.

May the road rise to meet you
May the wind be always at your back.
May the sun shine warm upon your face.
And rains fall soft upon your fields.
And until we meet again.
May God hold you in the hollow of his hand
May the Irish hills caress you
May her lakes and rivers bless you.
May the luck of the Irish enfold you.
May the blessings of Saint
Patrick behold you.

May your thoughts be as
glad as the shamrocks
May your heart be as light as a song.
May each day bring you bright happy hours,
That stay with you all year long.
For each petal on the shamrock
This brings a wish your way
Good Health, Good Luck, and Happiness
For today and every day.

Like the goodness of the five
loaves and two fishes,
Which God divided among
the five thousand men.
May the blessing of the King who so divided
Be upon our share of this common meal.

An old Irish recipe for longevity;
Leave the table hungry.
Leave the bed sleepy.
Leave the table thirsty.

IF YER IRISH
IRISH TOASTS

Here's to a long life and a merry one.
A quick death and an easy one.
A pretty girl and an honest one.
A cold beer and another one!

May those who *love* us love us.
And those that don't love us.
May God turn their hearts.
And if He doesn't turn their hearts,
May he turn their ankles.
So well know them by their limping!

Health and a long life to you.
Land without rent to you.
A child every year to you.
And if you *can't* go to heaven.
May you at least die in Ireland.

Drink is the curse of the land.
It makes you fight with your neighbor.
It makes you shoot at your landlord
- and it makes you miss him!

Now sweetly lies old Ireland
Emerald Green beyond the foam,
Awakening sweet memories.
Calling the heart back home.

An Irishman is never drunk as long as
He can hold onto one blade of grass
and not Fall off the face of the earth.

IF YER IRISH
IRISH PROVERBS

Life is like a cup of tea, its all
in how you make it!

I complained that I had no shoes
Until I met a man who had no feet.

T'is better to buy a small bouquet
And give to your friend this very day,
Than a bushel of roses white and red
To Lay on his coffin after he's dead.

Firelight will not let you read fine stories
but its warm and you won't
see the dust on the floor.

A trout in the pot is better
than a salmon in the sea.

If the knitter is weary the baby
will have no new bonnet.

The best way to keep loyalty in
a *man's* heart is to keep
money in his purse.

Humor to a man is like a feather pillow.
It is filled with what is easy to get
but gives great comfort.

Many an Irish property was
increased by the lace of a
daughter's petticoat.

There's no need to fear the wind
if your haystacks are tied down.

A wild goose never reared a tame gosling.

A boy's best friend is his mother
and there's no spancel stronger
than her apron string.

If you lie down with dogs,
you'll rise with fleas.

An old broom knows the dirty corners best!

To the raven her own chick is white.

It's no use carrying an umbrella
if your shoes are leaking.

There'll be white blackbirds before
an unwilling woman ties
the knot!

Irish Sayings and Proverbs

• WHAT'S GOOD FOR THE GOOSE
IS GOOD FOR THE GANDER.

• THE OLDER THE FIDDLE
THE SWEETER THE TUNE

• IT'S NO USE BOILING YOUR
CABBAGE TWICE

• DO NOT MISTAKE A GOATS BEARD
FOR A FINE STALLIONS TAIL

• THERE NEVER WAS AN OLD SLIPPER
BUT THERE WAS AN OLD
STOCKING TO MATCH IT

• AS THE OLD COCK CROWS
THE YOUNG COCK
LEARNS

• HUMOUR TO A MAN IS LIKE
A FEATHER PILLOW
IT IS FILLED WITH WHAT IS EASY TO GET
BUT GIVES GREAT COMFORT

• A NARROW NECK KEEPS
THE BOTTLE FROM
BEING EMPTIED IN ONE SWIG.

• IT'S FOR HER OWN GOOD THAT
THE CAT PURRS

• EVEN A TIN KNOCKER WILL SHINE ON A
DIRTY DOOR

• ONE BEETLE RECOGNISES ANOTHER

• WHEN THE SKY FALLS WE'LL
ALL CATCH LARKS

• ANY MAN CAN LOSE HIS
HAT IN A FAIRY-WIND

• IF YOU HAVE ONE PAIR
OF GOOD SOLES IT'S
BETTER THAN TWO PAIRS
OF GOOD UPPERS

• IT'S DIFFICULT TO CHOOSE
BETWEEN TWO
BLIND GOATS

• A SILENT MOUTH IS SWEET TO HEAR

• IT'S AS HARD TO SEE A WOMAN CRYING
AS IT IS TO SEE A BAREFOOTED DUCK

• HE'D OFFER YOU AN EGG
IF YOU PROMISED
NOT TO BREAK THE SHELL

• IT'S A BAD HEN THAT WON'T
SCRATCH HERSELF

• NO MATTER HOW OFTEN
A PITCHER GOES TO

THE WATER IT IS BROKEN IN THE END

* THERE WAS NEVER A SCABBY
SHEEP IN A FLOCK
THAT DIDN'T LIKE TO HAVE A COMRADE

* A NOD IS AS GOOD AS A
WINK TO A BLIND
HORSE

* THE FOX NEVER FOUND A
BETTER MESSENGER
THAN HIMSELF

* WHEN THE DROP IS INSIDE
THE SENSE IS OUTSIDE

* SHOW THE FATTED CALF
BUT NOT THE THING
THAT FATTENED HIM

* A BUCKLE IS A GREAT
ADDITION TO AN OLD
SHOE

* IN WINTER THE MILK GOES TO THE COWS
HORNS

• MEN ARE LIKE BAGPIPES
NO SOUND COMES
FROM THEM TILL THEY'RE FULL

• SNUFF AT A WAKE IS FINE
IF THERE'S NOBODY
SNEEZING OVER THE SNUFF BOX

• YOU MUST CRACK THE
NUTS BEFORE YOU CAN
EAT THE KERNEL

• EVERY PATIENT IS A DOCTOR
AFTER HIS CURE

• NEITHER GIVE CHERRIES
TO PIGS NOR ADVICE
TO A FOOL

• SOFTWORDS BUTTER NO PARSNIPS
BUT THEY WON'T HARDEN
THE HEART OF THE
CABBAGE EITHER

• YOU'LL NEVER PLOUGH A
FIELD BY TURNING IT
OVER IN YOUR MIND

• THERE ARE FINER FISH IN
THE SEA THAN HAVE
EVER BEEN CAUGHT

• A TYRONE WOMAN WILL
NEVER BUY A RABBIT
WITHOUT A HEAD FOR FEAR IT'S A CAT

• A WINDY DAY IS NOT THE
DAY FOR THATCHING

• THE OLD PIPE GIVES THE
SWEETEST SMOKE

• MARRIAGES ARE ALL HAPPY
IT'S HAVING BREAKFAST TOGETHER THAT
CAUSES ALL THE TROUBLE

• A SCHOLARS INK LASTS LONGER THAN A
MARTYRS BLOOD

• TAKE GIFTS WITH A SIGH,
MOST MEN GIVE TO BE PAID

• A TURKEY NEVER VOTED FOR AN EARLY
CHRISTMAS

• WHAT BUTTER AND WHISKEY
WILL NOT CURE

THERE'S NO CURE FOR
- THE IRISH FORGIVE THEIR
GREAT MEN WHEN
THEY ARE SAFELY BURIED

- THE LONGEST ROAD OUT
IS THE SHORTEST
ROAD HOME

- A MAN LIVES LONG IN HIS NATIVE PLACE

- IT IS BETTER TO BE ALONE
THAN TO BE IN BAD
COMPANY

- IT IS NOT A SECRET IF IT
IS KNOWN TO THREE
PEOPLE

- THERE ARE TWO SIDES TO
EVERY STORY AND A
HUNDRED VERSIONS OF EVERY SONG

- AN EARLY RISER GETS
THROUGH HIS BUSINESS

- THE PERSON OF THE
GREATEST TALK IS THE
PERSON OF THE LEAST WORK

- GIVE THE PRIEST HIS OWN
SIDE OF THE ROAD

- A LIGHT HEART LIVES LONG

- YOU MUST LIVE WITH A
PERSON TO KNOW A
PERSON

- THE MAN WHO WON'T TAKE
ADVICE WILL HAVE
CONFLICT

MY OWN COLLECTION OF POEMS

"These poems were written during a few weeks in July around 2002. I think and I consider them to be my best work."

- GERRY CASEY

A CAPTURED DREAM

Forever in a dream,
Of unending passion of throes,
Where limitations
Have no obvious limitations,
And time stands still,
Captured in stationary episodes,

Surveyed in minute detail,
Of beauty unsurpassed,
Then is released once more,
Into earthly timescales,
And the dreams remembered,
In every split-second that occurs.

Gerry Casey

Going Home.

I can see the house now
Memories of Childhood
How great they've been
Our car trundles up the path,
Of varied stone,
Oh for a hot cup of steaming coffee,
To warm my chilled bone,

I've been away so long,
A little frightened of my return,
On foreign pastures,
I've had my bridges to burn,

The autumn leaves fall
Reluctantly to the ground,
As they fondly envelope the path,
I know that I am homeward bound,

I shudder at the welcome,
I may receive,
Many things have happened,
I now concede,

The car grinds to a halt outside the house,
Standing so tall and proud,
I faintly knock on the door, full of fear,
My head bowed, yet hopeful.

Gerry Casey

Note....

Moments

Look then at spectacular moments;
moments that come aglow and go,
Episodes that reveal something
worthwhile that shows,
Fading moments buried in time
that are difficult to recall,
Moments that mean something
precious that say it all,

Emotional moments that rob the soul
of vigor and color it with rigor,

Often false, often real, impinging
on a nerve, making one feel,
Moments of tenderness, moments of
sorrow, but there is always tomorrow,
Moments of optimism, moments of
hope, brought to fruition by one's
intuition, bringing about new dawns,
full of vibrancy, expectation,
A new tomorrow of joy unsurpassed.

Gerry Casey

Watershed

Remove all traces of prejudice,
ignorance and resentment,
Hatred, anger and violence, let it all go,
Substitute warmth for coldness,
love for hatred, understanding for
ignorance, openess for prejudice,
peace for war, joy instead of anger,
Happiness for sadness,
optimism for pessimism,
A new dawn has arrived,
no more shed blood,
Over the horizon, it beckons so
clear; unity amongst people of
every shade, faith or creed,

Effort, will and sustenance are
needed; it's our only chance.

Gerry Casey

Immersed in Detachment.

Observing a spectacular infusion of
splendour richness and sparkling light
transforming into saturated bronze
like foilage arriving at a crescendo of
pulsating, replenishing moisture, protecting
golden nuggets enclosing undiscovered
secrets, remaining elusive to countless
generations, going back to misty eras that
captured a kaleidoscope of enchanting
spell binding imagery, glimmering,
glancing, and perpetually persuasive.

Pearls of wisdom containing abstract
discoveries unbeknown to humankind
that may unravel ancient secrets that were
lost in the unfettered haste of modernity,
shackled by concepts such as industrial
revolutions and advanced technology
of material components, but absent of
substance, spirtituality and meaning.

Gerry Casey

Nocturne Activity.

Neon lights, shades of black and
white, absorbed in city life.
Club bars predominately red, bright beams,
people in search of unrequited dreams,
Money changing hands, deals
done on the spot,
Similar phenomena dating
back to the year dot,
The night is young and will eventually
transcend into another day,
Bar stools high, sit strategically
in neat position,
People perched aloft, money at the ready;
perhaps a cure for their thoughts,
A kaleidoscope of colored
cocktails, red, green and blue,
And every hue, but still the void remains.

Gerry Casey.

Sunsets.

I love sunsets, those dramatic, breath-
taking moments when all of your cares
dissipate in a golden release of worldly
pleasure that makes life worthwhile.

The sunset at that moment adds precious color and fleetingly splendor to the utmost drab of settings that unites the poor and the rich in that currency is not required, as if God lets loose that brilliant sunshine to everyone irrespective of wealth or class.

Those golden rays are meant to be of equal value to all. Not for the privileged few but for all of the peoples of the planet and perhaps as a consolation for those who do not nor intend to prosper financially as some who do but who may not appreciate a golden sunset as those who have time to do so?

Gerry Casey

Natural Selection.

Where at once the straw colored fields
meander into distant horizons,
And contrast with the huge blue sky
of the picturesque landscape,
Where many species of birds
dart in undulating fashion,
Chattering in a cacophony of
orchestrated melody,

Looking down at easy pickings on the
vast blanket of golden cornfields,
Focusing on targets and careering
down with unerring accuracy,
Gliding downwards with effortless
ease to make their selections,
Choosing with precision and returning
to safety of the blue laden skies.

Gerry Casey

WORDS

Words that speak, Words that flow
Words that mean, Words which glow
Words of courage, Words of fame,
Words of worship, Words the same.
Words that were richly spoke
Words that make some men choke
Words that we could not do without
Words that mean sincere
and Words of doubt.

Gerry Casey

People

People laughing, people singing,
People losing, people winning,

People good and people bad,
People happy and people sad,
People crying, people sighing,

People surviving, people dying,
People here, people there,
People troubled, people with care,

People working, people not,
People idle, people left to rot
People.....

Gerry Casey

TYPICAL LURGAN CHAT
(Explanations in brackets
where appropriate)

Ye cuddn't lack im if ye reared
im. *(I don't like the guy)*
He's a nice wee man when he's sleeping.
Cuddn't ye titter! *(Couldn't you but laugh)*
I cud laugh at im.

Wise up. *(Come to your senses)*
As sound as a pound. *(Honest)*
As straight as a die.
Least said, easiest mended.
As God made them, he matched them.
If you get the name of an early-
riser, you can lie all day.
(False reputation)
Like getting blood out of a stone.
Up to all the tricks in the book.
The green-eyed monster. *(Jealousy)*
He'll get his day of it. *(When one
does a bad turn on another)*
Laughing all the way to the bank.
He sounds like a cracked record.
He'll just have to lack it or lump it.
*(When something is not altogether
pleasing to an individual)*
The evil eye. *(Referring to a person
or an animal such as a cat)*
Hell hath no fury like a woman scorned.
The early bird catches the worm.
Empty vessels make the loudest noise.
You'd have to be up early to catch her out.
I wish I had your oul sock.
*(Referring to someone suspected
to have lots of money)*
I wish I was a pound behind you.
(Again someone well-off)

More money than sense.
New light from an old window.
(*Someone who has reputedly
underwent a personality
transformation*)

SAM'S GOLDWYNISMS

One of the most prolific exponents of the catch phrase or colorful remark was Sam Goldwyn, the celebrated American Film Producer.

Born in Warsaw, Poland in 1882, he arrived in the U.S. penniless at the young age of 15 years. His original name was Schmuel Goldfisz, but when he presented himself to the immigration official on arrival, his name sounded like Samuel Goldfish and this is what he become known as. He later changed from Goldfish to Goldwyn after joining forces with Edgar Selwyn to form a film corporation called Goldwyn, which was an amalgamation of both names. Afterwards the same company became famous as Metro-Goldwyn-Mayer. At the time, the slogan for the corporation was the studio with more stars than there are in heaven.

Sam Goldwyn specialised in a *'film of the book'* format and among his many successes were **'Bulldog Drummond'** (1929) and **'All Quiet on the Western Front'** (1930). **A** groundbreaking creation of his was the musical **'Guys & Dolls'** (1955) where Marlon Brando had a singing role, much to the film world's surprise. Other notable productions were **'Dead-End'** (1937) starring a young Humphrey Bogart and **'Wuthering Heights'** (1939) with Lawrence Olivier winning international acclaim for his performance.

When Sam emigrated to the States at 15, he could barely speak a word of English. However, like everyone else he managed to scrape through and survive, becoming a successful businessman in the process. Throughout his renowned career in the film industry, he continually astounded people with his witty out of context colourful remarks. Whether this was a deliberate ploy to confuse, bewilder and to bewitch the populace, is open to interpretation. Taking into consideration that he hadn't the privilege of English tuition, like most American children of his generation, he may in fact genuinely have had life-long problems with the language. Likewise as a film supremo and astute businessman that he was, he may have been employing a unique brand of wordplay to amuse and bemuse people at their own expense. Either way, a sampling of his sayings have been as popular as some of his huge successes on the Silver Screen and have been immortalized and incorporated into the English language.

Probably his most famous saying has been: *"Gentlemen include me out"*, on resigning from the Motion Picture Producers and Distributors of America in October 1933. His catch phrases caught on so much that they became famous as Goldwynisms, thus adding a new dimension to the English language.

I suspect a lot of his *'grammatical errors'* were indeed intentional, as Sam apparently had a *'wicked'* sense of humour and loved to get one over on people. His humorous ways and witty persona obviously paid off, as Sam passed away in 1974 at the grand old age of 91, leaving behind an amassed fortune of some $4million. Not bad for someone who *'couldn't get to grips'* with the English language!

THE SAYINGS OF
SAMUEL GOLDWYN

☞ This makes me so sore it gets my dandruff up.

☞ A verbal contract isn't worth the paper it's written on.

☞ Gentlemen, include me out.

☞ In two words, I'm possible.

☞ We've got to take the atom bomb seriously. It's dynamite.

☞ We're overpaying him, but he's worth it.

☞ Anyone who goes to see a psychiatrist ought to get his head examined.

☞ Let's start with an earthquake and work up to a climax.

☞ If I could drop dead right now, I'd be the happiest man alive.

☞ Tell me, how did you love my picture?

☞ Anything that man says you've got to take with a dose of salts.

☞ The reason why so many people showed up at Louis B Mayer's funeral was because they wanted to make sure he was dead.

☞ My horse was in the lead coming down the straight, but the caddie fell off.

☞ Why only twelve disciples? Go out and get thousands.

☞ Going to call him 'William'? Every Tom, Dick and Harry's called William. Why don't you call him 'Bill'?

☞ If you can't give me your word of honor, will you give me your promise?

☞ A wide screen makes a bad film twice as bad.

☞ When an actress complained that a film director was sadistic, Sam said, *"It isn't true. He's just a very mean fellow."*

☞ I'll think of something. Call me tomorrow and remind me what it is.

☞ I don't think anybody should write his autobiography until after he's dead.

☞ I never put on a pair of shoes until I've worn them at least five years.

☞ Our comedies are not to be laughed at.

☞ You just don't realise what life is all about until you have found yourself lying on the brink of an abscess.

☞ That's the way with these directors; they are always biting the hand that lays the golden egg.

☞ Pictures are for entertainment; messages should be delivered by Western Union.

☞ Why should people go out and pay to see bad movies, when they can stay at home and see bad television for nothing?

MISQUOTED

Things that famous people were
said to have said, but didn't
actually say it!

BEAM ME UP, SCOTTY.

An ubiquitous remark that Captain Kirk was supposed to have used when requesting to be returned from a planet to the Starship Enterprise. *"Beam us up, Mr. Scott"*, is in fact the nearest equivalent found.
GENE RODDENBERRY 1921 –91 'Star Trek'.

ELEMENTARY, MY DEAR WATSON.

Not found in any book by Conan Doyle. Although a review of the film 'The return of Sherlock Holmes' *in New York Times 19th October 1929 states,* "In the final scene, Dr. *Watson* is there with his 'amazing Holmes' and Holmes comes forth with his Elementary, my dear Watson, elementary". *The nearest to this in Doyle's own work is,* 'Excellent', *I cried.* 'Elementary', *said he.*
**ARTHUR CONAN DOYLE 1859-
1930 – The memoirs of
Sherlock Holmes (1894)**

England and America are two
countries divided by a common
language.
Attributed to this and other forms
to George Bernard Shaw.
However, not found in Shaw's
published writings.
GEORGE BERNARD SHAW 1856-1950

It is necessary only for the good
men to do nothing for evil to
triumph.
Associated with Edmund Burke,
but not found in his work.
EDMUND BURKE 1729-97.

***MAN, IF YOU GOTTA ASK,
YOU'LL NEVER KNOW.***
*When asked what jazz was, Louis
Armstrong actually said,*
"If you still have to ask.... Shame on you".
**LOUIS ARMSTRONG 1901-71:
MAX JONES SALUTE TO SATCHMO (1970)**

ME TARZAN, YOU JANE.
*Summing up his role in Tarzan,
The Apeman (1932 film):*
"The words occur neither in the
film nor the original, by Edgar

Rice Burroughs".
**JOHNNY *WEISSMULLER* 1904-
84 in Photoplay Magazine
June 1932.**

PLAY IT AGAIN, SAM.
In the film Casablanca, Humphrey Bogart says,
"If she can stand it, I can. Play it!".
Earlier in the film Ingrid Bergman says,
"Play *it* Sam. Play as time goes by".
**JULIUS J EPSTEIN 1909 –
CASABLANCA -1942 Film)**

**WHY DON'T YOU COME UP
AND SEE ME SOMETIME?**
*Alteration of her invitation in the
film* 'She done him wrong'.
She in fact said, "Why don't you
come up sometime and see
me?".
**MAE WEST 1892-1980: She done
Him Wrong (1933 film)**

YOU DIRTY RAT!
Associated with James Cagney, but
not used by him in any film.
In a speech at the American Film
Institute Banquet, 13th March

1974, Cagney said, *"I never said
mmm, you dirty rat!"*.
JAMES CAGNEY 1899-1986
Cagney by Cagney (1976)

FAMOUS SAYINGS BY EMINENT MEN

"If you take the game of life seriously
If you take your nervous system seriously
If you take your sense organs seriously
If you take the energy process seriously
You must turn on, tune in and drop out".
A Lecture, June 1966 in The Politics
of Ecstasy (1968/Ch. 21)
TIMOTHY LEARY American Psychologist.

Love and sorrow twins were born
On a shining showery morn.
- THOMAS BLACKLOCK (1721-1791)

Didst thou but know the only touch of love,
Thou would'st as soon go
kindle fire with snow
As seek to quench the fire
of love with words.
- SHAKESPEARE

A loving heart is the truest wisdom.
- DICKENS

Let me not to the marriage of true minds
Admit impediments. Love is not love
Which alters when it alteration finds,
Or bends with the remover to remove:
Oh no, it is an ever-fixed mark,
That looks on tempests,
and is never shaken:
It is a star to every wandering bark,
Whose worth's unknown
although his height be taken;
Love's not Time's fool, though
rosy lips and cheeks
Within his bending sickle's compass come;
Love alters not with his brief
hours and weeks
But bears it out e'en to the edge of doom:
If this be error, *and* upon me proved,
I never writ, nor no man ever loved.

- SHAKESPEARE

THE BALLAD OF
MASTER McGRATH

Eighteen sixty-nine *be* it ever renowned,
McGrath and his keeper they
left Lurgan town,
A Gale from the wind it soon
wafted them o'er
And the 18th they landed on Albany's shore.

And when they came to that
fair coursing *groun'*
The gentlemen present they
all gathered round,
Some one of the *party* did raise a 'Ha, *Ha*'
Is this the great dog you
call Master McGrath?

Lord Lurgan speaks up and
says he, "Gentlemen,
If there's any *of youse* has
got money to spen'
For the sportsmen of England
I don't care a straw,
Five hundred to one on my
Master McGrath".

The Master looked up and he
wagged his long tail,
He seemed to know what
his lordship did mean,
"Bet on noble lord and don't fear them *ava*,
I'll solve them a problem",
says Master McGrath.

The game was got ready with
caution and speed,
The judge he was mounted
upon a grand steed,

When the dogs was unslipped
the whole crowd did Hurra!
The pride of Old England
against Master McGrath.

Poor Puss he led them on
as swift as the wind,
Sometimes Bob was before
and sometimes behind.
Bobby took the first turn, according to law,
And the second was awarded
to Master McGrath.
As Bob and the Master were going along,
Bob asked him, "What took
you so far from home?
You'd have been better off in
your heathery demesne
As to come and gain laurels
on our Altcar plains.

"It's true," says McGrath, "we've
gran' heather bogs.
But in our town of Lurgan we
have good men and dogs".
He quick led the van and
the crowd did Hurra!
"Snuff that up your noodle",
says Master McGrath.

Poor Puss led them on, t'was
a beautiful view,
You'd have thought over the green sward
Like lightening they flew.
McGrath pounced upon her
and held up his paw,
"Three cheers for old Lurgan",
said Master McGrath.

Now you sportsmen of England,
in future beware.
Though I emptied your purses
your honours I bear,
But be kind to poor Bobby
when I'm far awa,
Until the next time he meets
Master McGrath.

**Written by "The Bard of
Silverwood," Henry McCusker.**

EDUCATION
(LURGAN STANDARDS)

As thick as two short planks.
Brains to burn.
If they had brains, they would be dangerous.
Doesn't know his ass from his elbow.

As cute as a barn owl.
Thinks he knows everything.
A know all who knows nothing.
Empty vessels make the loudest noise.
A smart ass.
He knows his onions. *(Not necessarily a greengrocers).*
More in his head than a comb would take out.
Knows more than his prayers.
Wasn't born yesterday. *(Perhaps the day before).*
Hasn't a clue.
Is that upside down or downside up?
Wud argue a black crow white. *(But wrongly).*
Not the gospel truth.
An ignorant man!
What wud ya expect from a pig – but a grunt?
People in glass houses shouldn't throw stones.
He cuddn't read nor write.
Money talks!
A smart wee man.
Brains are better than brawn.
Not as green as he's cabbage luckin.
Knows what side his bread's buttered.
He's no mug!
Not as daft as he lucks!

FOOTNOTE: Some sayings may overlap or be repeated. This is unavoidable as certain sayings fit certain categories more often more than once – Author.

MARGORIE McCALL

**Lived once,
buried twice.**

Lurgan in Co Armagh is renowned for the birthplace of A.E. Russell the great poet, painter and contemporary of Yeats. Also that great greyhound *'Master McGrath'*, owned by Lord Lurgan, had a song composed in his honor and became part and parcel of folklore in the town.

However probably the most bizarre and fascinating tale to come from the town is that of the legend of Margorie McCall who is recalled as the woman who lived once, but was buried twice. The story goes that in or around the first half of the eighteenth century, a lady by the name of Margorie McCall who resided with her husband in one of the little houses in Church Place between 'The Holy Family Reading Room' and 'The Commercial Hotel' was pronounced *'dead'* and a few days later interred in Shankill Graveyard. At the time of her supposed demise she had on one of her fingers a very valuable gold ring, which her family had vainly tried to remove. Consequently, they had to make the unfortunate decision to allow the ring to go with her to the grave. Some knowledgeable thief became aware of this fact and was determined to avail himself of the booty. This was a common occurrence in that era. Having opened the grave, he then proceeded to prise open the lid of the coffin. He then attempted to cut off the finger, which wore the ring with his knife, in order to secure the jewelry. As he drew blood, to his astonishment and utter bewilderment, Margorie arose from her coffin and confronted him. The perplexed grave robber got the shock of his life and fled from the cemetery, panic stricken, never to be seen again. Meanwhile, the grief-stricken husband of Margorie was sitting forlornly at home, mourning the loss of his beloved wife. Suddenly a knock was heard at the door, 'Ah', he said, 'If Margorie was alive I would swear that was her knock'. For it seemed to be Margorie's usual unique knock. Something urged him to go to the door. He was amazed to find Margorie standing there, adorned in her grave clothes. Overcome by emotion and shock, he immediately fainted on the spot. Soon he recovered and to his delight and utter amazement he realized that his beloved wife had been restored to him, although only yesterday he had attended her funeral and burial. For some years afterwards they continued to live happily together and had a son who became a clergyman. Eventually Margorie finally died, naturally this time, and was interred in Shankill Graveyard for the second and last time.

At her grave was placed a stone that recorded the fact that she had been buried twice, with the date of each interment. A similar occurrence happened in Charlottetown in Canada as did other reporting's worldwide. It was actually referred to as a '*resurrection*' in those days.

The actual grave and tombstone of Margorie McCall can to this day be seen in Shankill Graveyard, although it has been vandalized on various occasions.

GERRY CASEY

INTERNATIONAL SAYINGS
OF THE 90'S

ZBIGNIEW BRZEZINSKI 1928 –
U.S. Secretary of State and National Security Advisor.
"Russia can be an empire or a democracy, but it cannot be both".
In foreign affairs March/April 1994
"The Premature Partnership".

BARBARA BUSH 1925-
Wife of George Bush (Sen): First Lady of the United States 1989-93.
"Somewhere out in this audience may even be someone who will one day follow in my footsteps and preside over the White House as the President's spouse. I wish him well!"
At Wellesley College Commencement – June 1990.

ERIC CANTONA 1966-
French Footballer, Ex, Man.Utd.
"When seagulls follow a trawler, it is because they think

sardines will be thrown into the sea".
*Stated to the media following a
press conference 31st March
1995.*

**BILL CLINTON 1946-
42nd President of the U.S.A. from 1993.**
"I experimented with marijuana
a time or two. I didn't like it –
I didn't inhale."
Washington Post – 30th March 1992.

THE COMEBACK KID! –
His own description of himself
after coming 2nd in the New
*Hampshire primary in the 1992
Presidential Election.*
(Since 1952, no presidential
candidate had won the election
without first winning in New Hampshire).

**ROBERTSON DAVIES 1913-95
Canadian Writer.**
"It's an excellent life of somebody else. But
I've really lived inside myself and she can't
get in there."

*From his interview in the Times 4th April 1995 –
commenting on a biography of himself.*

JOSEPH HELLER 1923-
American Novelist.

"When I read something - saying I've not done anything as well as Catch-22, I'm tempted to reply. Who Has?"

DAVID HOCKNEY 1937-
English Artist.

"The thing with high-tech is that you always end up using scissors".

ALIJA IZETBEGOVIC 1925-
President of Bosnia.

"And to my people, *I* say this may not be a just peace, but it is more than just a continuation of war".

After signing the Dayton accord with representatives of Serbia and Croatia.

In Dayton, Ohio 21st November 1995.

GARRISON KEILLOR 1942
American Humorous Writer.

"Years ago, manhood was an opportunity for achievement and now it is a problem to be overcome".

FRAN LEBOWITZ 1946-
American Humorous Writer.

"The best fame is a writer's fame: it's enough to get a table at a good restaurant, but not enough that you get interrupted when you eat".

PAUL McCARTNEY 1942-
Beatle Singer/Songwriter.

"Ballads and Babies – that's what happened to me".
On his 50th Birthday.

CANDIDA McWILLIAM 1955-
English Writer.

"With the birth of each child, you lose two novels".

DENNIS POTTER – 1935-94.
Writer/dramatist: Author of
the Singing Detective.

"Religion to me has always been the wound, not the bandage".

YITZHAK RABIN 1922-95
Israeli Prime Minister 1974-7 + 1992-5.

"We say to you today in a loud and clear voice: enough of blood and tears. Enough."

To the Palestinians at the signing
of the Israel – Palestine
Declaration
In Washington, 13th September 1993.

**RONALD REAGAN 1911-
40th President of the U.S.A. 1981-
9. Former Hollywood
Actor.**
"I now begin the journey that will
lead me into the sunset of my
life".
On revealing to the American people
that he was suffering from
Alzheimer's disease.

THREE TIMES A CHAMPION

'Master McGrath', the famous greyhound who has succinctly encapsulated Lurgan Town. According to Lurganite dialect, *"He was some pup."*

Enter Master McGrath, the legendary greyhound, who was to go on to make history by becoming the first greyhound to win the Waterloo Cup on no less than three occasions.

The dog was owned by the 2nd Lord Lurgan of the Brownlow Family, who were instrumental in the evolution of Lurgan as a thriving town, both historically and commercially. Lurgan's success as a linen trade metropolis owed much to them.

The story goes that, in or around, 1865, Lord Lurgan, a renowned figure in coursing circles, owned a kennel and hunting lodge at Calling near Dungarvan in Co. Waterford. The estate was managed by a James Galway. Lord Lurgan then sent his sire '*Dervock*' to be mated with '*Lady Sarah*,' a coursing dam.

Later, a litter of pups were born which included a rather unpromising looking individual. In the following weeks, the pup appeared to be making little, if any, progress and Mr. Galway had decided to put the pup down. The kennel lad by the name of McGrath had become attached to the pup and pleaded with Mr. Galway to let him look after it.

Later, when the dog was around 14 months old, he created a sensation by winning a race at a meeting run by the Halfway Coursing Club in Waterford.

As the word got around, people doubted that such a dog was the property of a kennel boy. Eventually, it emerged that the rightful owner was Lord Lurgan. A sum of money changed hands and soon the dog was on its way to Lurgan to be trained by John Walsh at Brownlow House. The dog was given the name of **'MASTER Mc GRATH**.

Regarding the conformation, people over the years have been quoted as saying he was the perfect greyhound in looks. However, according to his trainer, John Walsh, this was not the case, quite the opposite in fact. In his words, Master McGrath *"was a little 54 pound dog with a sour looking, plainest head. He would look up at you as if he owned the universe. He had a good killing neck that ran into plainest shoulders. His chest was fairish depth, but he had a wonderful spring of rib and the best muscled back I ever saw."*

From that description, we can deduce that *"The Master"* had a mixture of good and bad qualities. A rare combination in a greyhound. Nevertheless, one that meant he was destined to go on to be a world-beater in every sense of the word.

In October 1867 at Raughlin, Master McGrath made his first appearance in the north when he won the Visitors cup which had an entry of 32 dogs.

The following year he was entered for the Waterloo Cup at Altcar in England. He readily defeated 'Cock Robin' in the final to become the first Irish greyhound to win the coveted title.

In 1869, he repeated last year's success when he defeated 'Dabs-at-the-Bowster' in the final to capture a brace of Waterloo Cups.

In treacherous, icy conditions, the following year, Master McGrath was eliminated in the first buckle. He nearly came to grief when he fell into the river Alt. Luckily; he was rescued by his slipper, by the name of Wilson.

It was reported in the press that several leading families in Lurgan lost a fortune on the race, and indeed had to pawn the deeds of their estates in order to settle debts to English bookmakers.

After the race, a stunned Lord Lurgan declared that the dog would never race again. After a period at stud, the dog took his place again in the Waterloo Cup at Altcar in 1871. He impressively won the race for an unprecedented third time and so became a national hero.

Lord Lurgan, Lord-in-waiting to the Queen in 1869-74, was invited by Queen Victoria to present the famous dog to her. Unfortunately, the great dog died in 1871, in the year of his greatest triumph. After rumors circulating that the dog had been poisoned, Lord Lurgan sent the carcass to Trinity College in Dublin. After a post-mortem, it was revealed that the dog died from double pneumonia. It was also disclosed that Master McGrath had a heart, half as large again as the average greyhound.

At the home of the Earl of Cardogan at Culford Hall, near Bury St. Edmunds, a monument erected by Lord Lurgan stands proudly, with the following inscription:

Though thrice the victor at *Altcars'* plain
McGrath's fleet, limbs can never win again
Say man, thy steps, the dog's memorial view
Then run the course honest and true.

So ends the story of **'Master McGrath'** a legend then and still a renowned *'famous son'* of Lurgan and part of the history and fabric of the town. If we ever see the likes of him again, we will indeed be fortunate.

Gerry Casey

A Brief Glossary to explain some of the terminology contained in the book for the benefit of non-Lurgan readers.

CUD (CUD'NT) .... COULD/COULDN'T
WUD (WUD'NT), ...WOULD/WOULDN'
LACK...LIKE
AFF .... OFF
YER .... YOUR
MUN .... MONEY
GIT .... GET
GITTING............................... GETTING
TILL..UNTIL
BATE .... BEAT
LUCKS .... LOOKS
DISN'T .... DOESN'T
QUARE ....GREAT
MA.. MY
DACENT ....DECENT
CRATUR................................... CREATURE
TAY .... TEA
ANAW....................................... ANOTHER
PACE .... PEACE
SOWL ....SOUL

WIREY...STRONG
LUCK1N... LOOKING
WAA .... WEATHER
OUL ....OLD
KEN...CAN
DUN.. DONE
WOARKING ....WORKING
LILTY.................................... FIT AS A FIDDLE!

SMILE AWHILE

Traffic Warden: Why are you
driving with a *bucket of*
water on the passenger seat?
Motorist: So *I* can dip my headlights.

How did the baker get an electric shock?
He stood on a bun and a
current ran up his leg.

Gerry: We had a burglary last
night and they took
everything except the soap and towels.
Terry: The dirty crooks.

Passenger: Will this bus take me to Belfast?
Driver: Which part?
Passenger: All of me, of course!

A man was in court charged with parking his car in a restricted area. The judge asked if he'd anything to say. 'Well, they shouldn't put up such misleading notices', the man said. It said: 'Fine for Parking Here.'

THE OLD SCHOOL LIST

In clearing out the rubbish
Of an attic long disused,
I found, securely tucked away,
A scrapbook much abused.
And, turning o'er its pages,
With their corners thumbed and worn,
Found names of schools and classmates
I had loved in day's agone.
The list is long, and doubtless
One a stranger's eye would spurn,
But those who knew and loved them,
I am sure will gladly turn,
And once again go through it,
Finding names, as close they look,
That long had lain forgotten
in the folds of memory book.
From fancy's rolls I call them,
And a far-off echo fills
My soul with eager longing
As the old-time answer thrills,

And the old-time rafters ring
To the same old rhythmic flow
That bound in love
The comrades of sixty years ago.

But many ne'er will answer
To an earthly call again
The roll above is growing
While the few who here remain
Are waiting, glad to answer 'Present'
On the other shore,
Glad to be again enrolled
Among the friends of yore.

High Hopes

He thought he could do it but blew it,
He thought he could climb to
the top of the steeple,
And shout down to the people,

Before he could catch his breath,
He slipped and near fell to his death,
He was saved by the buckle on his belt,
As he came tumbling down showing his pelt,

Coming down, he dived to his left
and amid a sharp shower,

He careered into the bell tower,
Thud!!
He began to quote from the bible,
And peeped down to see Harry Twyble
'Cud you help me Harry, I've fallen asunder'.
'Well' said Harry 'The forecast
is for thunder!'

'Hells bells' he cried. It'll be raining cats and dogs next,
'I'll have to light a wee fire in here to keep me warm,
'I'm freezing that much I'll end up in the funny farm!'

'Tell somebody to throw me a rope, I'll use me buckle and pray to the pope, Sure I'm no dope. I'll get there without any oul saft soap, Then I might elope with yer woman down the lane, six months with me and she'll go insane and the two of us will get a wee flat in the Caribbean.'

Let's get back to the rope folks, and the people, and the steeple.
The people have formed a crowd and threw me a rope,

I've attached the buckle and everything is looking fine and dandy and I can now have a wee chuckle.
Down I go swinging high and low; I'm swaying up and down and around,

The buckle has moved a notch and its playing havoc with me watch,
Its two minutes fast and the rope may not last,
There's a crowd down below on a 24 hour fast,
I must release the friggen belt, but gravity directs me back to the steeple,
The entire population of Lurgan is out to watch this flaming fiasco,
As I do figures of eight due to mismatch of belt and rope.
Never again will I climb the steeple to talk to the people,
Eventually I'm rescued. I thank God who calls me a sod and I go back to the people.

Gerry Casey

Vincey's Adventures. by Gerry Casey

Vincey Lavery has many a story to tell. Always good for a laugh, affable and friendly, you are lucky to get a word in edgeways when in conversation with Vincey and the fact that I am equally guilty of talking too much means that it usually results in a real jousting match when the two of us are having a chin wag!

Nevertheless, It's always good craic when listening to accounts of Vinceys' life and he is also an Everton fan like myself which means we can return to football now and then when things may get a bit boisterous! Vincey was a popular taxi driver in Lurgan until recently. Due to ill health, he reluctantly decided to park his taxi and give his vocal chords a rest (only kidding son!) for the foreseeable future!

I was very surprised and indeed interested to know that Vincey was once employed as an 'extra' appearing in some famous TV shows such as Minder. He has done the usual café scenes where perhaps Arthur Daley and Terry McCann were contriving some crafty scam!

He tells me that when an extra is engaged in a café scene, you were required to mime and appear to be anonymous as you could because if you were really chatting away, it would interfere with the sound effects and therefore disrupt the main players when they were shooting a typical scene.

Being an extra may be surplus to requirements, you may say! It was easy money according to Vincey and a chance to 'bump into' some celebrated stars of the small and big screens.

This brings me to Paul McCartney who was a member of probably the most famous group of all time, the Beatles. Both Vincey's daughter and his ex-wife have met the great man on separate occasions. The first time was when Vincey's then wife took a tumble in the snow in Liverpool. Well, blow me away, didn't the rock idol pick her up from the icy pavement and as a bonus, gave her his autograph!

The second occasion happened when Vincey's daughter was shopping in a supermarket when she spied Paul doing some shopping of his own. Well I ask you! The besotted girl sprinted over to Paulo and asked for his autograph. What happened next! To her surprise, the Mull of Kintyre kid planted a great big smacker on Vincey's daughter, explaining that a great big kiss was better than an autograph! All together now readers!

Thank you Sir Paul! How much is a McCartney autograph on eBay these days? You can't sell a kiss, can you?

During his time as an extra, Vincey has met and worked with many famous celebrities, albeit as an extra and tells me he had a great time in doing so. John Thaw of Inspector Morse fame was one of them. Vincey said that he liked Thaw and that he was always the best of craic and forever telling jokes. One thing that I learned from Vincey was that Thaw, who everyone observed walked in an unusual way, actually contracted this through diphtheria, an illness, almost unheard of these days, but a potential killer then when John Thaw was a boy. Perhaps Thaw's unusual gait may have indirectly helped his career as he was original and stood out from the crowd?

Vincey also relates that Charles Bronson of 'Death Wish' fame was in real life as he starred in some films, aggressive, unfeeling and 'hard as nails', probably accountable to his own hardship in earlier character building days?

Once, a stunt man called Rocky fell to his death. The entire crew were stunned and in an awful state. However, Bronson remained aloof and seemingly unaffected, saying that was life and part and parcel of a stunt man's job. Perhaps they were the cruel facts of the game. However, one would have thought that Bronson would have shown some passion and sensitivity towards his fellow man. Perhaps some events require a certain amount of professionalism?

Yes, Vincey has some fascinating stories to tell. Unfortunately due to lack of space in this volume, I'm afraid that I cannot continue Vincey's adventures but there is always tomorrow.

Epilogue
Lurgan is more interesting than what first comes to mind. Allow the visitors make their own minds up. They might surprise us!